Brushing up on Grammar

"If language were set in concrete, there would be no call for new books on how to use it."

—Roy Blount, Jr.

Brushing Up on Grammar

An Acts of Teaching Approach

Joyce Armstrong Carroll, EdD, HLD
and Edward E. Wilson

A Teacher Ideas Press Book

LIBRARIES UNLIMITED

AN IMPRINT OF ABC-CLIO, LLC
Santa Barbara, California • Denver, Colorado • Oxford, England

Library of Congress Cataloging-in-Publication Data

Carroll, Joyce Armstrong, 1937–
    Brushing up on grammar: an acts of teaching approach / Joyce
Armstrong Carroll, Edward E. Wilson.
        p. cm.
    Includes bibliographical references and index.
    ISBN 978-1-59884-372-9 (alk. paper)—ISBN 978-1-59884-373-6 (ebook)
1. English language—Grammar—Study and teaching. I. Wilson, Edward E. II. Title.
    PE1097.C36 2010
    428.2071—dc22   2009051189

ISBN: 978-1-59884-372-9
E-ISBN: 978-1-59884-373-6

14   13   12   11   10   1   2   3   4   5

This book is also available on the World Wide Web as an eBook.
Visit www.abc-clio.com for details.

Libraries Unlimited
An Imprint of ABC-CLIO, LLC

ABC-CLIO, LLC
130 Cremona Drive, P.O. Box 1911
Santa Barbara, California 93116-1911

This book is printed on acid-free paper ∞

Manufactured in the United States of America

Dedicated to all the teachers who have attended the Abydos Grammar Camp and who in doing so helped us breathe life into the study of grammar. To Joan Mathieu who was kind enough to read the manuscript before we sent it to our publisher. To Sharon Coatney, our editor, and Ron Maas, VP of Libraries Unlimited, who continue to believe and support our work.

As always this book lives because of all the trainers, trainees, and teachers who breathe life into the Abydos Learning philosophy.

CONTENTS

WHAT'S IT ALL ABOUT, ALFIE?

> "Grammar is to a writer what anatomy is to a sculptor, or the scales to a musician. You may loathe it, it may bore you, but nothing will replace it, and once mastered it will support you like a rock."
>
> —Beatrice Joy Chute

The Five Meanings of Grammar

When we say the word *grammar*, most of us think there is one meaning, one sense shared by everyone. Actually that is not the case. In a seminal article entitled "Grammar, Grammars, and the Teaching of Grammar," written for *College English* and published in 1985 and subsequently published in *Acts of Teaching*, first and second editions, Patrick Hartwell identifies five meanings of grammar. Briefly summarized they are

Grammar one—Grammar in the "head"

These are the internalized patterns we assimilate from hearing the language around us. Part of our literacy learning, this is grammar without the rules.

Grammar two—Linguistics

Here we find the description, analysis, and formulization of formal language patterns—the formal rules.

Grammar three—Usage

This really isn't grammar at all but the way people use language. Affected by society, personal choices, time, and geography, this "grammar" is sometimes called linguistic etiquette in the sense that we refer to expressions such as "I am she" as good *grammar* and "Him and me went to the video arcade" as bad *grammar*. This is the part of language that evolves, as it is constantly changing. An interesting aside, usage falls in and out of acceptability. For example, the double negative once used by Shakespeare for emphasis is now considered "bad" or incorrect grammar.

Grammar four—School grammar

Quite literally this is the grammar taught in schools. But note that schools never teach all the Grammar Two formal rules.

Grammar five—Style

Here we manipulate language with a conscious attention to surface form.

This article clarifies the grammar picture for all of us—teachers, educators, parents. As Hartwell contends in his article, we need grammar to communicate in meaningful contexts, we need to be able to manipulate language for stylistic effect, and we need to develop an awareness of language. He argues for language to sit at the center of curriculum "not as 'necessary categories and labels' but as literal stuff, verbal clay, to be molded and probed, shaped and reshaped, and, above all, enjoyed" (Hartwell, in *Acts,* 2008, 403).

Knowing Grammar and Knowing About Grammar

Knowing grammar and knowing about grammar are, as they say, two different animals. Anyone reading Chute's quotation and comprehending it *knows* English grammar. Hartwell would call this the grammar in our heads, the grammar we assimilate just being alive and growing up in an English-speaking country, the grammar we know and use unconsciously.

Knowing *about* grammar is what Hartwell would call *school grammar*. This is the grammar we attempt to learn every year, year after year, in English classrooms but ultimately remain insecure about it. This is the grammar we use to write and analyze sentences, call a noun a noun, understand syntax, and call upon to talk about our writing. But this is the grammar most people loathe.

Brushing Up on Grammar is our attempt to provide a palatable resource for re-entering that classroom and brushing up on those skills never quite internalized or those that were internalized but have faded over time. This book is for teachers, educators, and parents who want a realistic and interesting rehearsal (to use Murray's term—a *re-hearing* [Murray 1968]) of the major grammar concepts. We punctuated most chapters with a teaching idea, which will help teachers and parents help younger learners.

Why Teach Grammar?

We staunchly believe two things about the teaching of grammar: it should be taught within the context of writing and reading; teachers need to know *about* grammar to be able to teach grammar daily in their classrooms within the writing and reading processes. We, and everyone else up on their research, know that assigning and assessing grammar exercises, or distributing worksheets, is not teaching grammar—it is covering it. Worksheets and exercises do not serve students who are entitled to teaching that helps them understand grammar conceptually. Teaching conceptually helps them work with grammar within their own writing so they realize English grammar is functional. Only then will English grammar connect, "take," and linguistically empower them.

Why Learn Grammar?

Grammar is foundational and grounding and basic. Foundational, it provides the structural relationships of our language, including pronunciation, meaning, and linguistic history. Grounding, there is great power and security in an Aristotelian sense of the doer and the action. Basic, it sets out a system of rules for generating all possible sentences. As educated people in an English-speaking society, we should know this domain of knowledge. We involve language in everything we do (and we are judged by how we use it); we cannot live without it.

Today there is great emphasis on what is called "academic language," the language used in textbooks, classrooms, lectures, evaluations, for theories, and on tests. Grammar is intrinsic to the academic language of English. Differing in structure and vocabulary from the grammar in our heads, students who know the technical vocabulary of school grammar, usage, linguistics, and style are enormously more prepared to discuss in deeper, more literate ways, not only their writing but also the writing of others. Grammar is as much a part of the discipline of the academic language of English as literary, rhetorical, or figurative terms. How often do we discuss the elements of an essay, for example, compared to how often we use a subject, verb, or object?

Most importantly this opening rationale addresses what grammar does for us. The more we know about it, the better our variety, our strength, our flexibility with language. As Chute says, it will support us like a rock. When we learn English grammar within a meaningful context, it heightens our awareness of language and that awareness heightens our speaking, writing, and reading ability, not only by turning literate acts into better practice—correctness—but also by helping us use language more effectively.

Make no mistake: the effective use of language is power.

The ABCs of Grammar or Grammar's Six Characteristics

Over the years we have culled six characteristics that best describe grammar: It is abstract, borrowed, conventional, dynamic, elemental, and functional.

A = Abstract

We always say everything is a metaphor but the thing itself. This book is concrete, but the minute we draw a book

fig. 1.1

we have moved the concreteness of the actual book one step up the ladder of abstraction. If we write the word *book,* we moved two steps up that ladder. But if we refer to *book* as a noun, we have totally abstracted it. No longer is book the actual book but rather a term applied to book. So clearly grammar is meta-linguistic; it is language about language, and it is abstract.

Being abstract makes learning grammar difficult. Underdeveloped for most students until their early twenties, the frontal lobe of the brain has difficulty with abstract concepts. This is not to say that students can't grasp grammar concepts—rather teachers and parents must begin with the concrete and scaffold each grammar concept, moving from the concrete to the abstract. Rote memorization of the definition or filling in blanks does not work. When students realize that they are partaking in mindless repetition, they begin to dislike it, avoid it, and often just won't do it. Claiming grammar boring, students end up loathing it. The answer, one Carroll explored in *What Makes a Master Teacher,* is to bring the wonders down. Master teachers don't just tell students what to do; they show them. They model, model, model. They turn tiny mustard seeds into grand lessons and they make grammar interesting, challenging, and even fun.

B = Borrowed

Anyone who has taken a history of the English language course knows that English grammar was fashioned upon Latin grammar. Then that Latinate grammar traipsed into Old English with some grammatical changes to make it fit, to Middle English with more changes, through Elizabethan English with many changes. Today that grammar rests sometimes comfortably, sometimes uncomfortably, in our contemporary life. Yet residues remain. The "never split an infinitive" is an artifact from Latin where the infinitive is one word and cannot be split, for example, *ama* means "to love." Arcane spellings such as *oxen* retain an inflected ending long-gone but bedevil those who want consistency in spelling—*oxes*. Yet in many ways we are richer for the history of our grammar.

Richer, too, for all the borrowed words that pepper our prose and poetry. Booker T. Washington once said, "We don't just borrow words; on occasion, English has pursued other languages down alleyways to beat them unconscious and rifle their pockets for new vocabulary." Because so much of our language is borrowed and continues to be borrowed from other languages, English has an inconsistency in sound, spelling, and sense.

"Words can be fast travelers," Charles Cutler reminds us in *The English Language: From Anglo-Saxon to American* (47). Twitter, once only bird chirping or rapid, agitated, excited speech, now refers to the immediate posting of people's daily activities and thoughts. Within the space of one year, technology and the majority of people under the age of thirty throughout the world added not a new word but a new meaning to our lexicon. Our rich and varied lexicon comes from all over the world, both ancient and modern. Helping students learn and appreciate the grand variety of sources that enrich the English language is as much a lesson in cultural diversity as a lesson in vocabulary or lexical virtuosity.

C = Conventional

We cannot escape the conventions of grammar so needed for clarity. Knowing where to put a comma, when to indent, how to structure a phrase within a sentence, why a capital letter is needed makes for clear coherent writing. To say it another way, without conventions our meanings would muddle.

D = Dynamic

English is constantly changing, so we call it a living language. Dictionaries are updated all the time with new words, some borrowed—Have you eaten a *shawarma* yet? New meanings for existing words sometimes give us a tussle or a delightful double entendre, so we have to study the context—Is *cowboy* a romantic hero of the Wild West or a reckless person? Then there are all those connotations—Do we go to a beauty *parlor,* beauty *salon,* or beauty *spa?*

Carl Sandburg captured this dynamic nature of language in his poem:

Languages
There are no handles upon a language
Whereby men take hold of it
And mark it with signs for its remembrance.
It is a river, this language,
Once in a thousand years
Breaking a new course
Changing its way to the ocean.
It is mountain effluvia
Moving to valleys
And from nation to nation
Crossing borders and mixing.
Languages die like rivers.
Words wrapped round your tongue today
And broken to shape of thought
Between your teeth and lips speaking
Now and today
Shall be faded hieroglyphics
Ten thousand years from now.
Sing—and singing—remember
Your song dies and changes
And is not here to-morrow
Any more than the wind
Blowing ten thousand years ago.

E = Elemental

Grammar, the heart of language, the core of communication, the key to understanding the way meaning is expressed and the how it is interpreted, cannot be dismissed. To dismiss the need to study grammar is akin to dismissing the need to build a foundation for a house. Without a foundation a house will eventually collapse; without grammar our use of language will eventually falter.

F = Functional

Parts of speech or what some grammarians are now calling *word classes* often undergo grammatical conversions, which influence their function and meaning. Shakespeare started it all when he set one part of speech into the function of another. Rhetoricians call this *antimeria* or *anthimeria*, changing the part of speech of a word to another part of speech as in making verbs from nouns. In Act I of *Romeo and Juliet,* during an exchange with Benvolio and Mercutio, Romeo says:

> For I am proverbed with a grandsire phrase,
> I'll be a candle holder, and look on.
> The game was ne'er so fair, and I am done.

Proverbed? We suspect some of us would smite a student with red ink if he or she took such liberties with words. Yet we do it all the time—*Google,* the proper noun is often morphed into *google* the verb as in "I googled Shakespeare for my research paper."

In the *New York Times Magazine* as recently as September 20, 2009, Ben Zimmer in "The Age of Undoing" writes

> On popular Web sites devoted to social networking, innovative verbs have been springing up to describe equally innovative forms of interaction: you can *friend* someone on Facebook; *follow* a fellow user on Twitter; or *favorite* a video on YouTube. Change your mind? You can just as easily *unfriend, unfollow* or *unfavorite* with a click of the mouse" (18).

Let's look at the simple word *brown.* Most of us think of it as a color as in "He wore a *brown* suit." Clearly *brown* in that sentence is an adjective describing the color of the suit. It tells us the color of the suit and by inference what color it is not. It is not black or white or any other color; it is brown. That's why we say adjectives *modify* nouns.

If we capitalize the word as in "James *Brown* is the 'God-father of Soul,'" we see that the adjective *brown* has changed to a proper noun *Brown.*

But the word *brown* may also be a verb as in this imperative sentence: First, *brown* the meat in the pan before adding the spices. Easily, we see how changing the word class changes the function, which changes the meaning. And just as easily we see why contrived worksheets and grammar exercises, will never work the way re-entering our own writing or studying mentor texts will.

As we illuminated the five meanings of grammar and identified six characteristics of grammar—and there are others—we succinctly have stated the purpose of this book. While it is filled with categories and labels, rules and history, research and etymologies, we hope the examples and the connections help teachers and parents take our verbal clay to help students mold, probe, shape, reshape, and above all, enjoy their acts of language.

• Remember:

Grammar is our rock.

Teaching Idea

An absolutely splendid long-term project for students is to finish the ABCs of grammar by making an ABC Book of Grammar. What words would they cull to continue this alphabet? Perhaps they would choose G for Gerund or discover Graphology? This assignment challenges students to read and research, apply and synthesize. It fosters creativity and higher-level thinking and it's fun to share at the end of the unit or term.

IN THE BEGINNING WAS THE WORD:

WORDS, WORDS, WORDS

> "Words differently arranged have a different meaning, and meanings differently arranged have different effects."
> —Blaise Pascal

We take words for granted. After all, we have been saying them since babyhood, haven't we? But words are complicated little (and sometimes big) bits. They have parts that help convey their meaning, they have characteristics that enhance or change their meaning, they have history, and they have a classification. Additionally, our lexicon—the term itself coming from the Greek *lexis,* meaning *word*—is massive, conservatively somewhere between a quarter of a million to three-quarters of a million words.

First, though, let's look at the tiniest bits that make up words.

What Constitutes a Word?

We all know that letters come together to make words, but those letters and their combinations have names. As teachers, educators, and parents, we should be familiar with these terms. Let's review them.

Phoneme

A phoneme is the smallest *sound* in the language, e.g., the *b* in *bat*. Generally scholars agree that English has forty phonemes. This single fact is what makes phonics so difficult. We have more sounds than letters in our alphabet.

Morpheme

A morpheme is the smallest unit of *meaning* in the language. A morpheme is free if it can stand alone, or bound if it is used alongside a free morpheme. The word *unbeatable* has three morphemes: *un-*, a bound morpheme; *beat*, a free morpheme; and *-able*, a bound morpheme.

Grapheme

A grapheme is a fundamental unit in *written* language. Each grapheme corresponds to one phoneme, e.g., there are two graphemes in the *written* word *at;* three in the *written* word *fat;* three in the *written* word *chat.* The word *chat* has three graphemes because the *ch* in the spoken word represents one phoneme. See what we mean about phonics?

Lexeme

A lexeme is a unit of meaning, which exists regardless of the number of words it may contain or any of its parts. For example, each of the following is one lexeme: *dog, dog days, dogged, doggerel, hot dog, dog in the manger.*

Affixes

An *affix* is a *morpheme* added to a word to change its function or meaning. There are three basic ways to do this:

Prefix

Adding a morpheme to the beginning of a word may change its meaning. For example, the word *possible* becomes negative by adding the prefix *im-*: *impossible*.

Suffix

Adding a morpheme to the end of a word may change its function. For example, the adjective *cheerful* becomes the adverb *cheerfully* by adding the suffix *-ly*: *cheerful/cheerfully*.

Infix

Some languages add morphemes to the middle of the word, but this system is rarely used in English, except in expressions such as *fan-freakin'-tastic*. This insertion process is known as *tmesis*, which comes from the Greek "to cut" because the word is literally severed in two.

Root words

The base word, e.g., *move,* is the root or base word in *moved, moving, remove, removed, immoveable, moves, movies,* and so forth.

Denotation and Connotation

Now let's consider the figurative language of words through denotation and connotation.

Denotation

Denotation is the word's definition. Denotation is sometimes called *referential* or *cognitive language*.

Connotation

Connotation embraces the extension of words, their secondary or accompanying meanings. Connotation is sometimes called *emotive language* or *intension* to include all the nuances, feelings, implications, and inferences.

"Them-Nyms"

Some of "Them-Nyms" (a handy term coined for over twenty -*nyms* by Alana Morris in her book *Vocabulary Unplugged*, 29) are synonyms, antonyms, homonyms (homophones and homographs), and heteronyms.

Synonyms

Synonyms are different words (or sometimes phrases) with identical or very similar meanings. Words that are synonyms are said to be synonymous, and the state of being a synonym is called synonymy. The words *car* and *automobile* are synonyms. Similarly, if we talk about a *long time* or an *extended time, long* and *extended* become synonymous because they have the same connotation.

Antonyms

Hartwell considers antonyms under "Grammar Two," linguistics, because in lexical semantics antonyms are words in an incompatible binary relationship as opposite pairs (itself an oxymoron). For example: *front:back; long:short; up:down* are antonyms. What makes these words incompatible is that one word implies that it is not the other word; consequently, something *long* implies it is *not short.* Antonyms are in a "binary" relationship because there are two words. The relationship between opposites is known as *opposition.*

Homonyms

Homonyms mean same (*homo-*) name (-*nym*). Homonyms have come to include homophones (same sound) and homographs (same spelling).

> Homophones are words that have the same (*homo-*) sound (-*phon*) but different meanings and usually different spellings: *add* (addition), *ad* (advertisement); *bait* (lure), *bate* (to decrease); *plain* (simple), *plane* (flat surface), and so forth.

> Homographs, meaning same (*homo-*) write (*graph*), are words that are spelled the same but have different meanings and different origins: *angle* (shape formed by two connected lines), *angle* (to fish with a hook and line); *smack* (slight taste), *smack* (open lips quickly), *smack* (small boat), *smack* (to hit), to name a few.

Heteronyms

Heteronyms literally mean different (*hetero-*) names (*-nym*). Heteronyms are homographs that are pronounced differently:

> *affect* (influence), *affect* (pretend)
> *console* (cabinet), *console* (ease grief)
> *invalid* (disabled person), *invalid* (not valid)
> *minute* (sixty seconds), *minute* (very small)
> *wind* (air in motion), *wind* (turn).

To complicate matters, Sandra Wilde in *You Kan Red This!* (15) wonders whether calling attention to homophone pairs simply confuses us. She references Frank Smith (1982) who contends that we often misspell words not because we can't remember the right spelling but because we can't forget the wrong one. That may be the case when we try to remember *which witch* is *which?* That may ring true as we battle the choice between *frays* or *phrase.* How many of us have looked up *affect* and *effect* more than once or found ourselves thinking *does the word envelope with that e̲ tacked on the end mean the holder for a letter—the noun—or does envelope mean surround—the verb?*

Multi-Meaning Words

Also creating havoc are meanings that have morphed over centuries—or even over decades. What a word meant in the Elizabethan age, for example, often holds a different meaning today or holds its original meaning *and* a new meaning, causing readers to moan, "This doesn't make sense."

Classic sticky wickets such as "how she might *tongue* me" in *Measure for Measure* IV, iv, 27, which refers to a tongue-lashing or a harangue causes giggles in a high school classroom. The word *screw* in *Macbeth* Act I, vii, 59–61 "*screw your courage to the sticking-place*" generates outright guffaws.

So when words change over time in English, we can blame the Bard who took great liberties with words, thus paving the way for English to be a functional language. Always we must determine what a word means through its context.

Just today at lunch, our bilingual assistant asked about the word *miss*. So common is this word to us, we had to stop and think about it a minute. We offered

---

miss—as in longing for someone or some place;
miss—as to be too late for something;
miss—as in not hitting a ball with the bat;
Miss—as the title of a young lady.

Then we looked up *miss* in our unabridged dictionary. We discovered we *missed* "to fail to accomplish, achieve, or attain a goal," "to leave out or omit," and "to let something go by" as in to *miss* an opportunity. There are also the idioms: *miss a beat, miss fire, miss out on,* and *miss the boat.* Such a simple word but so much depends upon how it is used, its context.

Part of the reason we have multi-meaning words at all is because as we say in chapter one, English is a borrowed language. This brief list of animals illustrates this borrowing. Following the word is its original language and its original meaning.

---

tiger—Persian, arrow
elephant—Greek, ivory
giraffe—Arabic, long-necked
mosquito—Spanish, little fly
alligator—Spanish, *el lagarto,* the lizard.

Etymology

Words have a history just as we do, and that history adds to the word's meaning. We call this history a word's *etymology*. Etymology gives the background of a word in one or more of the following ways:

- by tracing its origin to its earliest recorded occurrence in the language where it is found
- by tracing its transmission from one language to another
- by analyzing it into its component parts
- by identifying its cognates in other languages
- by tracing it and its cognates to a common ancestral form in an ancestral language.

Let's look at the word *etymology* itself. *Etymology* comes from Middle English *ethimologie*, from Anglo-French, from Latin *etymologia*, from Greek, from *etymon* meaning the literal meaning of a word according to its origin, and *-ologia -logy* meaning a branch of knowledge. The word dates back to the 14th century.

Weather phenomena yield interesting etymologies:

storm—Old High German, stir
gale—Old Norse, yell, furious
cyclone—Greek, moving in a circle like a serpent's coil
typhoon—Cantonese, great wind
hurricane—Spanish from the West Indies, evil spirit

Vegetable names seem self-descriptive in their original forms:

asparagus—Greek, swell, burst forth
broccoli—Italian, small sprout
cabbage—Old French, head
rhubarb—Russian, named for the river Rha where it grew
rutabaga—Swedish, root bag (Cutler 1968, 48).

We are fascinated with the etymology and derivation of words, but we have two favorites:

Reaching back as far as 1970, in a study of recognition memory, Goldstein and Chance suggest, "A word is a simple visual structure, a fairly small, unitary input with perhaps three coding systems available into which it may be filed: auditory, visual, and meaning" (241). So we learn words by hearing them, seeing them, through their meaning and our intent, or through a combination of these learning styles— in other words, in a context.

pajama comes from India and means "leg clothing"
barbecue, so popular in our home state of Texas, comes from the Haitian word *barbacoa.*

Originally a frame meant to lift a bed off the ground, it evolved to mean the frame used to roast meat. Finally, as we usually use the word, it means the roasted meat itself.

Unkind as this next remark may be, it shows how cavalier we are in our borrowing of words. Since the war in Iraq, Arabic words have filtered into our language. Not too long ago we overheard a high school sophomore say to a group of his peers, "Hey, look at that girl. Man! She needs to wear a burka."

Burqa, burkha, burka, burqua all come from the Arabic word for the outside clothing women wear to cover their entire body and face, except the eyes. In his use of this borrowed word, the young man euphemistically called the girl ugly. We wouldn't be surprised if in time the word *burka* eventually morphs into the word *ugly.*

Parts of Speech: Word Classes

Confucius once said, "If names be not correct, then language and society are not in accordance with the truth of things." We name things. When we put a name to a person, place, thing, idea, or quality, we claim it as our own and often frame it by putting it in a context. We remember a vintage *Lone Ranger* film. In one early scene, as this man is establishing his identity as the Lone Ranger, he spots a wild white horse in the distance, one he wants and needs. Slowly he walks toward the horse, talking gently to it. Standing next to the steed, the Lone Ranger quietly says, "Silver" as he places his hand upon the horse's head. In that single act, the Lone Ranger names and claims the horse as his own.

So, too, is the case with words. Once we name them, know them and their functions, we are able to claim them as our own. So we study *parts of speech,* to place the abstract nature of knowing into concrete language. We classify words according to the way they work, so we can talk about them. The rub is that we cannot always tell what class a word belongs to by merely looking at it. Rather we need to look all the way around it to determine its function.

In traditional grammar we have eight agreed-upon classes of words—noun, pronoun, adjective, verb, adverb, preposition, conjunction, and interjection. In understanding the parts of speech, their meaning and function become key. As we saw in the example above, knowing the definition of *brown* is one thing, recognizing its function in each sentence is quite another. In the following chapters we take an in-depth look at these parts of speech, these word classes.

Teaching Idea

Dictionary digging

One of the best ways to get students involved with words is through their history, by studying the background of their favorite word or words. Make this a lesson of discovery, not a laborious exercise.

- Together as a class or in small groups, students list two or three of their favorite words. Teacher contributes, too.
- Using the *Oxford English Dictionary,* a good unabridged dictionary, or the various dictionaries on the Internet, students look up the back story of their favorite word. Sometimes the date of the word's first recorded usage is given. Encourage them to find out something weird.

Following is a sample from a middle school student named Qua.

My word is *junk.*

On *Wikipedia,* I found that *junk* comes from the Chinese dialect of Fujian province. In the Fujian dialect, *zun* 船 (pinyin Chuán), means "ship" or "large sea-going vessel." This was pronounced *jong* in

---

Malay but *junco* in Portuguese. That's where we got the word. These junks date back to the 2nd century.

On the *Online Free Dictionary*, I found this "Word History":

The word *junk* is an example of the change in meaning known as generalization, and very aptly too, since the amount of junk in the world seems to be generalizing and proliferating rapidly. The Middle English word *jonk*, ancestor of *junk*, originally had a very specific meaning restricted to nautical terminology. First recorded in 1353, the word meant "an old cable or rope." On a sailing ship it made little sense to throw away useful material since considerable time might pass before one could get new supplies. Old cable was used in a variety of ways, for example, to make fenders, that is, material hung over the side of the ship to protect it from scraping other ships or wharves. *Junk* came to refer to this old cable as well. The big leap in meaning taken by the word seems to have occurred when *junk* was applied to discarded but useful material in general. This extension may also have taken place in a nautical context, for the earliest, more generalized use of *junk* is found in the compound *junk shop*, referring to a store where old materials from ships were sold. Junk has gone on to mean useless waste as well.

In my mother's *The American Heritage Dictionary of the English Language* (unabridged), it had the same word history as the *Online Free Dictionary,* but in the library, I found lots of different meanings for the word *junk*. In *Webster's Third New International Dictionary* (unabridged) it says that in England *junk* is a thick piece or chunk of something such as cold salt mutton. *Junk* is also part of the head of a sperm whale, trash, and a woman from Paris named Rose Thurburn coined the term "junk jewelry." The library dictionary says it comes from Middle English *jonke.*

Oh, yes, one more meaning—in slang *junk* is heroin.

My father told me that *junk* is sometimes what they call baseball pitches that are not fast balls, curve balls, or change ups. I also found out there are *junk bonds, junk mail, junkyards, junk art,* and we all eat *junk food.*

My little sister's *Macmillan Dictionary for Children* shows a colored picture of a Chinese *junk* from the early 1400s.

I really got into this, so I went to my super duper Rodale *The Synonym Finder* and found a bunch of words—many I didn't know but I know now: *trash, litter, garbage, rubbish, riffraff* (that's one for sure I didn't know), *raff, chaff, crap* (that one I did know—ha ha), *dreck, schlock, trumpery, refuse, culch, waste, leavings, left-overs, odd bits, bits and pieces, odds and ends, truck, castoffs, rags, tatters, castaways, rejects, discards, trifle, trinket, gimcrack, gewgaw* (my grandmother says this word all the time), *bauble.* For verbs it had: *put in file 13 or 17* (never heard of that!) *or the circular or round file, throw out or away, get rid of, can.* Adjectives were: *trashy, junky, crappy, worthless, no-good, cheap, shoddy, shabby, poor, inferior, second-class, second rate.*

We know every student wouldn't get so much out of digging into one word, but we also know this historical journey into a favorite word can be exciting, especially when students are allowed to tap technology, conduct interviews, and double check the word in the library. And they love to share this.

THE NAME GAME:

NOUNS AND PRONOUNS

> "The beginning of wisdom is to call things by their right names."
> —Chinese proverb

Nouns

L ittle children call *nouns* "naming words" because that is what they do—they label or name our world. The word comes from the Latin *nomen* and the Middle English *nowne*, both meaning *name*. Take, for example, the word *nomenclature*. It is easy to see its Latin root and easy to understand why scientists and artists use this word for naming things.

Words classified as *nouns* name

persons (*boy, Joan*),

places (*Six Flags, playground*),

things (*ball, Liberty Bell*),

ideas (*freedom, love*),

or qualities (*courage, beauty*).

Like ice cream, nouns come in different flavors:

they can be abstract (*hope*) or concrete *(tree)*;

they can be common (*school*) or proper (*Alberto Gonzales Elementary School*);

they can be compounded as one word (*bullfrog*) or compounded as two words (*Eiffel Tower*) or compounded and hyphenated (*hand-me-down*);

they can be masculine (*bachelor*) or feminine (*spinster*);

and some nouns are collective (*gaggle*).

Also like ice cream, which may be comfort food, a pick-me-up, a treat or reward to cool down on a hot day, nouns serve different functions such as:

Function	Example
• subject	The *bus* ran into a tree.
• direct object	The factory made *candy*.
• complement	Snakes are *reptiles*.
• object of the preposition	Ken walked into the *store*.
• indirect object	The pitcher threw the *catcher* the ball.
• appositive	Lisa, my *neighbor*, has a great garden.

We often refer to the following chart to keep nouns straight.

Nouns at a Glance
Forms, Functions, Categories
Forms

singular	*son*
plural	*sons*
one-word compound	*grasshopper*
two-word compound	*high school*
hyphenated	*mother-in-law*
possessive	*Irene's/dogs'*
gender	*sister/brother*

Functions

subject	*Mary* ran up the stairs.
direct object	Trey picked the *rose*.
complement	He became a *jockey*.
object of a preposition	The elephants roared inside the *tent*.
indirect object	She gave the *church* her money.
appositive	Stan, *the carpenter*, worked on the deck.

Categories

common	*flower*
proper	*Liberty Bell*
concrete	*ball*
abstract	*ideals*
collective	*gang*

Singular/plural nouns

Generally when we think of nouns, we think of them as singular

> *girl*

and plural

> *girls.*

Neat and tidy. But, as is the case in grammar, everything gets a bit messy because we have regular and irregular plural forms and tons of exceptions.

Most of the time we just add an *s* to a singular noun to make more, but sometimes if the noun ends in *s, z, ch, sh,* or *x,* we have to add *es*

> glass/*glasses*

> fizz/*fizzes*

> hunch/*hunches*

> stitch/*stitches*

> hoax, *hoaxes.*

Other times we have to look at the noun's ending. If it ends in a *y,* we change that *y* to *i* and add *es*

> baby/*babies,*

if it ends in *f* or *fe,* we might just add an *s*

> surf/*surfs,*

but many times we change the *f* or *fe* to *v* and add *es*

> elf/*elves.*

Then there is the whole issue with nouns that end in *o.* The truth is some add an *es*

> hero/*heroes,*

while others just add *s*

> taco/*tacos,*

and some can be either

> avocado/*avocados/avocadoes.*

If we are unsure, we look it up.

Some nouns are flat out irregular, forming the plural in bizarre ways, and we just need to remember how to pluralize them if use them often or look them up if we don't. Irregular plural nouns depart from the usual patterns of forming plurals, which is usually due to the derivation of the word. Nouns coming from Latin or Greek may end differently than words from Old or Middle English, and both may differ from those coming from French. Words such as

> *alumnus/alumni; hypothesis/hypotheses; appendix/ appendices; beau/beaux; child/children; criterion/ criteria; vita/vitae*

vary because of their etymology. Some are exceptions even to irregular patterns and we're not sure why—because

> *foot* is *feet*

but

> *boot* isn't *beet.*

We don't know why

> *moose* is *moose*

but

• Remember:

Most of us have no trouble with the singular and plural in speech; it's when we go to write them that the trouble arises.

Of course, the more we read and write, the more we work with words, the more we hear them, try them out, play with them, the more familiar we become with those patterns and those that defy patterns.

> *mouse* is *mice.*

By the way, the accepted plural of the computer mouse is

> *mouses.*

Some nouns are just stubborn. They don't change a bit for any reason:

> *deer, fish, sheep, means, offspring.*

Among the most amazing things we have discovered about writing a book—even a grammar book—are the fascinating facts we unearth. Through Mario Livio's book *The Golden Ratio*, we found out that some five millennia ago numbers larger than two were treated as *many* and were called *es*. So *es* could mean a multitude, all, or three. Linguists think that this mark of plurality remains as our plural suffix.

We love "One Big Happy." Rick Detorie, its creator, captures in only a few frames the typical philosophies of three generations: the kids, Ruthie and Joe; the parents, Ellen and Frank; the grandparents, Rose and Nick. In fig. 3.1, James, a neighbor, listens with expressive zeal as Ruthie, age six, "teaches" adjectives. Ruthie, the master of malapropisms, and

fig. 3.1 By permission of Rick Detorie and Creators Syndicate, Inc.

double entendres, doesn't quite get things straight and strays to nouns, especially those proper ones.

Possessive nouns

Possessive nouns do just what they say they do—they possess:

> *Abel's* car

> *Sophie's* dress

Just remember the possessive form of nouns shows ownership and is usually formed by adding *'s* to the noun. If the noun is singular and ends in *s*, add *'s*; if the noun is plural and ends in *s*, in most cases just add the apostrophe.

Appositives or nouns in apposition

The appositive reminds us of two typical second-grade girl friends. They stick close to each other; they are inseparable, holding hands and skipping in unison on the way to lunch or the bus. An appositive works that way, too; it is a noun or noun equivalent that sticks close to the noun that comes before it and renames it.

> Henry, *the custodian,* works at our school.

Here *custodian,* the appositive, renames *Henry.*

> Alice, *Ben's wife*, just had a baby girl.

Ben's wife, the appositive, sticks close to *Alice.*

Noun complements

Don't confuse *complEment* with *complIment*. The first completes (think of the two *E*s in **complEtE**); the second praises (think of the *I* in *praIses*). When we talk about a noun complement, we mean *complement* in the sense of completing. So a noun in the predicate part of the sentence following a linking verb actually completes something from the subject part of the sentence. We also call this noun complement the subjective complement, a predicate noun, or a predicate nominative. (We think having multiple names for the same function really confuses people but the truth is different grammar books use different terms.)

• Remember:

A complement is different from an object because it relates to the subject rather than to the verb.

> The movie was *Gone with the Wind.*

In this sentence the name of the movie, which is in the predicate but follows the linking verb *was*, is a predicate noun that completes the subject *movie* by giving its precise name. Hence it is called a *noun complement, subjective complement,* or *predicate noun.*

Nouns in direct address

When someone is spoken to eyeball-to-eyeball and called by his or her name, we identify that name as a *noun in direct address* and we set that name off by commas.

> *Miss Smith*, did you read my essay?

Can you almost scc Miss Smith's eyeballs?

> We believe, *dear readers*, this book will help you.

Can you almost hear us addressing you?

> Surprise! I cleaned my room, *Mom.*

No doubt about it, the pupils of Mom's eyes are wide with surprise.

Pronouns

Most people dismiss pronouns as mere substitutes because they replace a noun or a noun phrase—Maria/*she*; Uncle Victor/*he*. True, in most cases. But passels of pronouns have specific functions each with a specific name: personal, demonstrative, indefinite, interrogative, relative, intensive, reflexive, reciprocal, and possessive. Overwhelming? Not so fast. In Anne Lamott's book *Bird by Bird,* her father cautions her little brother not to be overwhelmed by a project on birds. The brother moans, "But there are too many birds!" To which the wise father responds, "Son, just take them bird by bird." We shall heed the father's advice and take the pronouns the same way—pronoun by pronoun.

Personal pronouns

Personal pronouns sub for nouns. They *stand in for* specific persons or things. *Pro* in Latin means "for," literally *pro noun* means "for a noun." We talk about personal pronouns as "persons"—first, second, third.

First person means the pronoun involves the speaker or writer:

> *I, me, my, mine, myself, we, us, our, ours, ourselves.*

Second person refers to the person being addressed:

> *you, your, yours, yourself, yourselves.*

Third person denotes anyone else:

> *he, him, his, himself, she, her, hers, herself, it, its, itself, they, them, their, theirs, themselves.*

Personal pronouns are generally categorized as singular:

> *I, me, you, she, her, he, him, it;*

or plural:

> *we, us, you, they, them.*

But because they come to us from a heritage of Old and Middle English, gender, number, and case influence them. That's what gets most people in trouble—not the pronoun but its agreement. So here's an easy way to keep things straight.

When a pronoun replaces the subject, use

> *I, you, we, he, she, it, they.*

The trick is to try out the pronoun in place of the noun.

> John plays basketball.

He plays basketball.
We never say:

> *Him* plays basketball.

Likewise, when a pronoun replaces the object—object of a verb or a preposition, or is in the objective case—use

> *me, you, him, her, it, us, them.*

> John threw the basketball to Martin and *me.*

We never say:

> John threw the basketball to Martin and *I.*

Teachers like Joan Mathieu offer this hint to students: Take out the other name so it reads

> John threw the basketball to me.

Never:

> John threw the basketball to I.

But rather:

> John threw the basketball to Martin and him.

We never say:

> John threw the basketball to Martin and he.

After the preposition *to* in the previous sentences, we wouldn't say Martin and *I* or Martin and *he* because *I* and *he* are in the subjective case.

In the objective case, we say:

> The fight was between Harry and *me*.

We use *me* because it is the object of the preposition *between*.

> Theresa gave *me* the apple.

We never say "gave I" because *me* is the indirect object of *gave*.

> The death hit *them* hard.

We never say "hit *we*" or "hit *they*" because the word *them* is the direct object of *hit*.

Which brings us to the "courtesy rule." We never put ourselves first—shoving to the front of the line, for example, is rude. Well, we don't put ourselves first in grammar either. We never say:

> *I* and my boyfriend had a fight.

We say:

> My boyfriend and *I* had a fight.

Both *boyfriend* and *I* are in the subjective case (subjects of the sentence) and because of the courtesy rule—we don't put ourselves first.

And we never ever say:

> *Me* and my boyfriend had a fight.

Although we hear that construction more and more in common usage, for example, Levi Johnston's *Vanity Fair* exposé "Me and Mrs. Palin." Know that it breaks two rules—*I* not *me* is in the subjective case and because of the courtesy rule. Those who break those rules often tell us much about themselves.

And we never never ever say:

> *Me* and *him* had a fight.

That is wrong on three levels: it breaks the courtesy rule, it uses the objective case for *him,* and it uses the objective case for *me* while both are in the subject part of the sentence. Eeek!

In Spanish there is an idiom *El burro primero*—"the donkey first." The English translation fits here, "never put yourself first." The gist of the idiom also fits, "You wouldn't go anywhere if you put yourself before the donkey!"

Demonstrative pronouns

Demonstrative pronouns do just that—they demonstrate; they show or point out someone, some place, or something that was already named. *This, that, these, those* are tricky because they are singular and plural; using them correctly depends upon the context.

This points to one person, place, or thing (singular) *near* the speaker.

That is also singular but points to something *at a distance* from the speaker.

These points to more than one person, place, or thing *near* the speaker.

Those is also plural and points to something *at a distance* from the speaker.

Examples:

> *This* (pen) isn't working.

> The speaker holds one pen.

> *That* (photocopy machine) needs work.

> The one photocopy machine in the office is located across the room from the speaker.

> *These* (books) are heavy.

> The speaker holds many books.

> The chairs for the picnic are in the auditorium. *Those* (chairs) need to be moved outside.

> The word *Chairs* is plural, and they are at a distance from the speaker.

Indefinite pronouns

We all know what *indefinite* means. Often we call undecided plans *indefinite*. Other times when things are vague, we say, "things are indefinite." Basically, *indefinite* means the same thing when it comes to pronouns. Indefinite pronouns refer to non-specific words. *All,* for example, could mean three, ten, or two thousand. Indefinite pronouns replace persons, places, things not defined, not exact, or not specific. But we must be careful because—here's that word *function* again—sometimes they may be used as adjectives.

Common Indefinite Pronouns
All, any, anybody, anyone, another, anything,
everybody, everyone, everything, many, nobody,
some, somebody, someone, few, one, several, other,
each, either, neither.

Few came to the party Mary hosted.

Few girls came to the party Mary hosted.

In the first sentence *few* is an indefinite pronoun simply pointing out that only a few people came to the party.

In the second sentence *few* is an adjective modifying the word *girls*.

William Carlos Williams tells us "so much depends upon a red wheel barrow. . . ." In grammar so much depends upon how the word functions in the sentence.

Interrogative pronouns

Interrogative pronouns are used to ask questions. There are five interrogative pronouns:

Who? What? Which? Whom? Whose?

Nothing could be easier.

> *Who* is coming?

Who is the subject pronoun.

> *What* time is it?

> *Which* movie do you want to see?

> To *whom* did you give the answer?

Whom is the object pronoun because it is the object of the preposition *to*.

> *Whom* did you invite to the party?

Although *whom* looks like the subject because it comes first in the sentence, it is really the direct object. *You* is the subject; *invite* the verb; *whom* is the direct object—literally

> You invited *whom* to the party?

Relative pronouns

We have a dandy children's book *The Relatives Came* by Cynthia Rylant. Relatives "up from Virginia," do lots of hugging, laughing, helping, fixing, and eating when they arrive for a visit. At the end of the day, they breathe together as they squeeze into every available bed. Relative pronouns are like the relatives in that book. Think of them as "up from Virginia," so they are dependent upon but related in some way to what came before—the folks they are visiting. Grammarians would say it this way: a relative pronoun introduces a subordinate clause and connects it to the independent or main clause, sometimes called its *antecedent.* Relative pronouns are

that, who, whom, whose, which.

I told you about the relatives *who* came up from Virginia.

In this sentence the *who* is the relative pronoun introducing the restrictive (necessary) dependent relative clause *who came up from Virginia* and connecting it to the main or independent clause *I told you about the relatives.*

Jamie sat on the bench *that* was nearest the schoolyard.

Jamie sat on the bench is the main clause; *that was nearest the schoolyard* is the dependent relative clause introduced by the relative pronoun *that.* The relative clause is related to the main clause because it tells the location of the bench. So the relative pronoun *that* connects the word *bench* to its location.

Replace *Jamie* with *Who* and the same explanation stands.

Who sat on the bench *that* was nearest the schoolyard?

• Remember:

A relative pronoun *may be found* in a question but an interrogative pronoun is *always found* in a question.

Reflexive and intensive pronouns

Reflexive and intensive pronouns are personal pronouns that end in *self* or *selves.*

Defining the words *reflexive* and *intensive* helps us understand how reflexive and intensive pronouns work. The word *reflexive* literally means "directed back on itself," so reflexive pronouns refer back to the subject of the sentence.

Personal Pronoun	Reflexive Pronoun
I	myself
you (singular)	yourself
you (plural)	yourselves
he	himself
she	herself
it	itself
we	ourselves
they	themselves

We gave *ourselves* plenty of time to write this book.

That is the reflexive use of the word *ourselves* because it refers back to *we*.

The word *intensive* literally means "extreme" so intensive pronouns emphasize by repeating the subject of the sentence. Obviously both should agree in gender, number, and case. To make things easy, reflexive and intensive pronouns are exactly the same words; they just function differently.

I, *myself*, am tired of all these pronouns.

By placing the word *myself* immediately after *I*, I intensify the subject.

Following are two more examples:

The boys ran *themselves* ragged during the three-legged race.

That is the reflexive use of the word *themselves* because it refers back to *The boys*.

Notice the placement of the pronoun when it is used to intensify or emphasize the subject.

The boys, *themselves*, ran ragged during the race.

• Remember:

Reflexive
pronouns
*are never
subjects.*

Here again the emphasis is on *the boys,* so *themselves* is intensive. This particular grammar construction comes in handy when emphasizing something during the crafting of a piece of writing.

Mary and myself are friends is grammatically incorrect because *myself* cannot be the subject. While we're on the topic of incorrect grammar, we remind everyone to expunge *hisself, theirselves, ourself, themselves, theirselves* from their vocabulary. These words do not exist.

The two reciprocal pronoun phrases

When Carroll enjoyed the lead in her high school musical *Seventeen,* she sang the song "Reciprocity" (Stange 1951). The verses define, explain, and give an example for the word *reciprocity* and in doing so define, explain, and give an example for reciprocal pronoun phrases.

Through the cute and peppy (although somewhat dated) song, the lyrics convey *reciprocity* as a mutual or cooperative interchange, a relationship. By giving the golden rule as an example, the meaning becomes crystal clear. There you have it. The two reciprocal pronoun phrases are nice to others. They express reciprocity, a two-way relationship, in tight prose:

---

each other and *one another.*

> Jane gave Matt an anniversary present, and Matt gave Jane an anniversary present.

This is a wordy sentence. By using the reciprocal pronoun phrase *each other,* the sentence becomes tighter. Knowing this also helps craft in writing.

• Remember:

Reciprocal pronoun phrases tighten writing.

> Jane and Matt gave *each other* anniversary presents.

> Jane loves Matt, and Matt loves Jane.

Again, this sentence is too wordy.

> Jane and Matt love *one another*.

Possessive pronouns

The important thing to remember is that possessive pronouns do not take apostrophes even though they show ownership. Because possessive nouns take apostrophes, everyone thinks possessive pronouns do. We call this "the misplaced apostrophe notion," and it gets everyone in trouble.

Possessive pronouns used alone are

> *mine, ours, yours, his, hers, theirs.*

> She told the children that the new computers were *theirs.*

Possessive pronouns used to modify nouns are

> *my, your, his, her, its, our, their, whose.*

> *My* desk is cluttered with papers and books.

> I am buying a new car, but I am not sure of *its* color.

Pronouns and their antecedents

The major problem with pronouns is their antecedents (Fancy Nancy says *antecedent* is a fancy word for agreement). The tried but true adage states that pronouns agree with their antecedents in gender, number, and case. In other words, the noun, phrase, or clause to which the pronoun refers and the pronoun should be the same gender (male/female/neuter), number (singular/plural), and case (subjective, objective, or possessive). This is why we need to know our grammar.

> Jack dropped *his* bucket.

> Jill dropped *her* bucket.

When correlative conjunctions (see chapter six) join a compound antecedent, the pronoun agrees with the nearest antecedent.

> Not only Jack but also Jill dropped *her* bucket.

When the antecedent is a collective noun, it takes the singular pronoun if it's thought of as a unit, but it takes a plural pronoun if the collection is thought of as individuals.

> The couple took *his* and *her* bucket up the hill.

Couple is a collective noun taken as a unit (think: "each one"), so it takes singular pronouns.

> The couple took *their* buckets up the hill.

Couple is a collective noun taken as individuals, so it takes the plural pronoun.

Indefinite pronouns usually take the singular pronoun.

> No one dropped *his or her* bucket.

Compound antecedents joined by *and* usually take the plural.

> Jack and Jill dropped *their* buckets.

Compound antecedents joined by *or* or *nor* usually agree with the nearer antecedent.

> Jack or Jill dropped her bucket.

> Jack nor the boys dropped their buckets.

The It's/Its Problem

Grammarians tell us *it's/its* is the most frequently made grammar mistake, so here's a surefire way to check the correctness of all *it's/its*.

To check between *it's* the pronoun contraction and *its* and the possessive pronoun simply read *it's/its* as two words: *it is.* If the sentence makes sense with *it is,* the pronoun contraction *it's* works, but if it doesn't, use the possessive pronoun *its.*

In the sentence

> *I am buying a new car, but I am not sure of its color.*

• Remember:

If one of the antecedents is singular and the other plural, it is best to put the plural one last to avoid the monster AWK!

Read:

> I am buying a new car, but I am not sure of *it is* color.

That doesn't make sense; it sounds wrong, so you know you don't need the contraction of *it is*, you need the possessive pronoun *its*.

So, bird by bird, we have completed the pronouns. Now on to the three *A*s.

A+A+A:

ADJECTIVES, ADVERBS, AND ARTICLES

> "The adjective is the banana peel of the parts of speech."
> —Clifton Fadiman

Adjectives

The word *adjective* comes from the Latin *adiectivus*, which means "to add to." That describes the function of adjectives to a T. When adjectives modify, qualify, or limit nouns or pronouns, they add to those nouns and pronouns, making them more exact or vivid. Simply put, they tell us more about a noun or a pronoun by giving us the size, color, number, description, or details that make the noun or pronoun clearer in our heads. Adjectives in English usually come before the noun. This is not the case in other languages. For example in Spanish the adjective usually follows the noun—*salsa verde* literally translates *sauce green*.

The *white* gardenias filled the vase.

White tells the color of the gardenias, and it appears before the noun *gardenias*.

Sometimes adjectives wait until after the verb to do their work. We call these *predicate adjectives* or *adjective complements* because they are in the predicate part of the sentence.

> Gardenias are *white.*

White is a predicate adjective or adjective complement because it follows the linking verb *are* and describes the subject of the sentence *gardenias.*

Adjectives do important work in writing because they help create images and help specificity, but good writers don't overwork them. Using a string of adjectives is not nearly as effective as choosing the exact noun or one precise adjective.

> The *beautiful, aromatic, large, round, blossoming, white* flower sits in the vase.

is not nearly as effective as

> The *gorgeous* gardenia sits in the vase.

Degrees of adjectives

Educated people hold degrees and have letters after their names. Carroll has two doctorates, so six letters follow her name: three letters name one doctorate; three name the second doctorate. When people refer to her formally, they use "Doctor" before her name because of her degrees.

Adjectives also hold degrees, so letters follow their names to show their degree: *-er* shows the comparative degree and is used to compare two things; *-est* shows the superlative degree and is used to compare three or more things.

Sometimes, instead of those letters attached to the end of the adjective, we use *more* or *most; less* or *least* before the adjective to show the degree—just as we use the title "Doctor" before a name to show degree.

An adjective without a degree is simply called the *positive* with no letters after its name or words before it. But once an adjective graduates to compare something, it gets a degree. Here's how it works.

The positive degree indicates the simple quality without comparison, relationship: *wise.*

> The *wise* teacher does not lecture her students; she models the lesson for them.

The comparative degree compares two persons, places, things, or ideas. It uses *-er* or the word *more* to make the comparison.

> *Wiser* than her older sister, Judy obeyed her parents.

The superlative degree compares three or more persons, places, things, or ideas. It uses *-est* or the word *most* to make the comparison.

> The *wisest* fairy godmother wished Cinderella the gift of good judgment. She was *most wise* of them all.

positive	comparative	superlative
tall	taller	tallest
big	bigger	biggest
red	redder	reddest

Examples:
In the anniversary bouquet, one rose is *red*, another one is *redder*, but the rest of the roses are the *reddest.*

Irregular adjectives

Then there are those pesky irregular adjectives. These adjectives do not form the comparative and superlative by adding *-er* or *-est* to the root or by adding *more* or *most*; *less* or *least.* Therefore, since their pattern deviates from the norm, they are called *irregular.* Lots of reading and writing helps get these into the long-term memory, but we remember memorizing them in "grammar school." Here are the most common:

bad	worse	worst
far (distance)	farther	farthest
far (degree)	further	furthest
good	better	best
ill	worse	worst
late	later	latest or last
less	lesser	least
little (amount)	less	least
many	more	most
much	more	most
well	better	best

Adjective complements

Adjectives used as a complement, a completing, are called *predicate adjectives*.

Some movies are *boring*.

The adjective *boring* following the linking verb *are*, is a predicate adjective or adjective complement because it completes the subject *some movies* by giving a general description of them.

• Remember this little rhyme:

If you can count the amount, use *fewer*; but for things in a mess, use *less*.

The less/fewer problem

Many misuse the adjectives *less* and *fewer* when comparing amounts of something.

Fewer refers to the countable number of individual things or persons, whereas *less* refers to the general quantity of something.

Fewer students graduated this year than last year.

Individual students can be counted both this year and last year and the numbers can be compared.

> *Less* water runs from the faucet since we added that new contraption.

While we can judge the quantity of water running from the faucet, we cannot count it.

The farther/further problem

Both of these adjectives are comparatives for the word *far*, which is why folks mix them up.

> Jim walked *farther* down the path as he considered his options *further*.

Here *farther* indicates distance whereas *further* indicates the abstract degree of his options.

The little/littlest/least problem

The adjective *little* has two meanings. *Little* is a multi-meaning word that can mean either size or amount.

> Christian is a *little* boy for a third grader.

Here the word *little* means Christian is small in size.

> Please give me a *little* piece of birthday cake.

Here the word *little* means a small amount.

So far, so good, right? Except things get muddier in the comparative and superlative degrees because *little,* meaning size, changes to *littler* and *littlest*. But *little,* meaning amount becomes *less* and *least.*

> Christian is *littler* than Joey.

● Remember:

Farther refers to physical length or distance—think *far*.

Further refers to abstract ideas, degree, something being added, time, or amount—think *fur*.

Here *littler is* in the comparative degree because Christian is compared to one other boy.

If *little* means size, it gets bigger in the comparative and superlative with -*er* or -*est.*

If *little* means amount, it actually shrinks when being compared— *less* and *least* have fewer letters than *little.*

Think of the film and TV show *Honey, I Shrunk the Kids* and shrink *little* when talking about amounts.

> Christian was the *littlest* boy in third grade.

Here *littlest* is in the superlative degree because Christian is compared to all the boys in third grade.

> Oh, please give me *less* cake than that.

Here the positive *little* refers to amounts, so *less* in this sentence means less than *that piece.*

> Give me the *least* amount of cake.

Here *little* is also an amount, so *least* in this sentence means the *least* amount of the whole cake.

When we read this "One Big Happy" cartoon, we knew that Detorie understands how kids often read those mindless, often incorrectly structured worksheets. Ruthie gives much thought to this fill-in-the-blank exercise, deciding upon *pretty* instead of *busy.* Piaget would have loved it. We loved it. A man just sitting on a tractor doesn't look busy to us either. So, responding to her mom's look of disbelief, Ruthie gives her six-year-old reason. We find that when students fill in these mindless worksheets, they try to make sense out of the sense-lessness of them. Besides, an urban six-year-old probably wouldn't even recognize a tractor!

fig. 4.1 By permission of Rick Detorie and Creators Syndicate, Inc.

Adverbs

Not too long ago we heard a fourth grader define adverbs for his teacher. Stunned by the simplicity and accuracy of his definition, we knew immediately he understood the function of adverbs. He said, "I think adverbs do with verbs what adjectives do with nouns." How great is that? Adverbs certainly modify verbs, but the neat thing is they can also modify everything else—adjectives, other adverbs, clauses, even sentences *but* not nouns and pronouns—that is the work of the adjective.

Tails vs. no tails

Adverbs are the "gossips" of language because they often tell *when, where, why, how,* or under *what* conditions something happens or happened.

Some folks suffer from an adverbial pseudo concept because they think all adverbs end in *-ly*. True, some adverbs have the *-ly* tail such as *frequently, quietly, nicely* but so do some adjectives such as *monthly* as in *monthly* payments, *holy* as in *holy* water, *friendly* as in *friendly* letter. Here again just looking at the word in isolation does not reveal its function. We have to always ask, "What is that word doing in the sentence?" Also, some adverbs do not have tails such as *how,* as in *How* are the children? *where,* as in *Where* is the meeting? *too,* as in She is *too* pretty to be real. *Very,* as in Coco's fur is *very* soft. These are called simple or flat adverbs because they have no tails.

• Remember:

When, where, and *why* are relative adverbs and introduce relative clauses.

Ruthie and James are back in fig. 4.2. This time Ruthie in her attempt to "teach" adverbs gives a typical Ruthie definition for them. James, ever the skeptic, doesn't buy it, to which Ruthie retorts with that killer of a clincher.

fig. 4.2 By permission of Rick Detorie and Creators Syndicate, Inc.

Degrees of adverbs

Like adjectives adverbs carry degrees. Like adjectives the degrees are *positive, comparative,* and *superlative.*

The positive degree

The positive degree expresses no comparison: *seriously.*

Sally *seriously* considered her schedule.

Seriously modifies the verb *considered* in its positive form.

The comparative degree

The comparative degree increases or decreases the positive form by comparing two things: *more seriously* or *less seriously.*

Bert *more seriously* considered his schedule than did Sally.

In this sentence Bert is compared to Sally so the adverb is comparative.

The superlative degree

The superlative degree indicates the greatest or least degree among three or more things: *most seriously* or *least seriously.*

Conrad, however, considered his schedule the *least seriously* of the three.

In this sentence Conrad is compared to Bert and Sally so the adverb is superlative.

Regular adverbs

Regular adverbs generally follow this rule:

---

if the words are one-syllable, add the *-er, -est* endings;

---

if the words are more than two syllables, use the words *more, most;*

if the words are two syllables, the writer/speaker has a choice.

one-syllable adverbs		
soon	sooner	soonest
more than two-syllable adverbs		
interesting	more interesting	most interesting
two-syllable adverbs		
able	abler	ablest
able	more able	most able

Irregular adverbs

Like adjectives, irregular adverbs change when moving to the comparative and superlative degrees.

The most common irregular adverbs

badly	worse	worst
badly	less badly	least badly
good, well	better	best
far	farther, further	farthest, furthest
little	less, lesser, littler	least, littlest
many, some, much	more	most

The good/well problem

Good is an adjective and *well* is an adverb. We do some-thing *well* but we give a friend something *good.* So when an activity is described, use the adverb *well,* but when a condition is described or if the choice follows a linking verb (refer to how to test for a linking verb in chapter five), use the adjective *good.* In other words, check the function—what do you want the word to do—describe an activity (verb) or a condition (noun)?

> Mary Jane paints *well.*

Since *paints* is an activity (verb), *well* is used.

> I visited the hospital and Scott looked *good.*

Looked describes Scott's condition, so *good* is used. *Looked* is also a linking verb (Scott *is* good) and takes the predicate adjective *good.*

> Jim is a *good* student.

Good is an adjective modifying the noun *student.*

The bad/badly problem

The same logic used for *good/well* holds for *bad/badly.* When it's an activity (verb), use *badly,* the adverb; when it's a condition (noun) or if it follows a linking verb (complement), use the adjective *bad.* How the word functions determines the choice.

> This season looks bad for the Rockets.

Looks describes a condition and is a linking verb (the season *is* bad for the Rockets), so the adjective *bad* is used.

> The tennis match ended *badly.*

Ended describes an activity, so the adverb *badly* is used.

Articles

A, *an,* and *the* are the three articles (technically adjectives) in English and they always keep company with nouns. *A* and *an* are indefinite because they escort indefinite or general nouns, whereas *the* is definite because it escorts definite or specific nouns.

> I looked at *a* car yesterday.

> I looked at *the* Porsche today.

In the first sentence *a* is used because car is indefinite—that is, not the name of a specific car. In the second sentence *the* is used because the car is definite, a Porsche.

> Mary picked *a* tomato and *an* herb from her garden.

• Remember:

If the noun begins with a vowel or any word that sounds like a vowel, for example, *honor*—notice the *h* is silent—use *an* not *a*—*an honor.* Based on phonetic rules, the choice of *an* removes the awkward momentary silent pause, called the glottal stop in the parlance of phonics, that *a* would require. For example, *an heir* is less awkward to pronounce than *a heir.*

SIMON SAYS:

VERBS AND VERBALS

> "Life is a verb."
> —Charlotte
> Perkins Gilman

Verbs

erbs, the powerhouses of English, drive the meaning, drive the sentence, drive the action, drive the mood, drive the tone, drive the time. We cannot overestimate their importance.

Action verbs

We all know action verbs show the action being done by the "doer" or the subject of the sentence:

run, jump, play, scamper.

The girls and boys *run* and *jump, play* and *scamper* about the schoolyard.

The *girls* and *boys* are the "doers" in that sentence. What they "do" is *run, jump, play,* and *scamper*—verbs, all.

"To be" verbs

Apparently action verbs are too easy, so some grammarian, with a weird sense of humor, came along and shook up things with another type of verb—verbs that show existence. We call these "to be" verbs:

> *am, is, are, was, were, be, being, been.*

No action but plenty of existence with these busy "bees."

We sprinkle "to be" verbs everywhere. Because the Greek god, Proteus, was capable of instantaneously changing like the sea, we call the "to be" verbs the most protean of the English language because they constantly change form. They are

Type	Example
irregular	*was/be*
linking	Las Vegas *was* fabulous
verbs of existence	She *was* a Girl Scout
passive	Alberto *was* questioned by the principal
progressive	I *was* going to the veterinarian when I saw him
used with adverbs	Salvador *was* always late
and overused	He wanted an appointment *that was* made with a doctor.

Teaching Action and Existence Verbs

An easy and fun way to distinguish action from existence verbs is to play "Simon Says." Playing this is not too elementary; the idea came from Shawn Bird, then a teacher in but now a principal at a middle school.

Invite the students to stand and then give the instructions. "Simon says wave your hands." They do. "Simon says nod your head." They do. "Simon says run in place." They do. "Simon says BE." The first time they stop, stock-still and stare, but as you continue to play the game with the other "to be" verbs interspersed among the action verbs, they get the concept—"to be" verbs show no action; they just show existence.

Linking verbs

Some verbs link. These tiny connections (called copulas) connect the subject of the sentence with more information about the subject. The following verbs are true linking verbs:

> *am, is, are, was, were, has been, are being, might have been, become,* and *seem.*

> Sylvia *is* happy.

Because "*is*ing" is not something Sylvia can do, the word *is* links the subject *Sylvia* to more information about her—happiness. In this sentence, *Sylvia* is the subject, *is* the linking verb, *happy* the predicate adjective or adjective complement because it describes the proper noun *Sylvia.*

Other linking verbs are schizophrenic because they may link or show action:

> *appear, feel, grow, look, prove, remain, smell, sound, taste, turn, stay, seem, become,* and *grow.*

> Sylvia *seems* happy.

Again, the linking verb *seems* links the subject *Sylvia* to more information about her.

Let's try that test on the following sentence.

> After the rain, Alfreda *felt* the damp wall in her house.

• Remember:

Here's a way to test if a verb is action or linking: just substitute *am, is,* or *are* for the verb (except for *appears*). If the sentence still makes sense, it is a linking verb.

> After the rain, Alfreda *am* the damp wall in her house.

No linking verb because the sentence doesn't make sense.

> After the rain, Alfreda *is* the damp wall in her house.

No again. Alfreda *is* the wall? We don't think so.

> After the rain, Alfreda *are* the damp wall in her house.

Two problems. The subject and verb don't agree, so it doesn't make sense.

After applying this test, we know in this sentence *felt* is an action verb, not a linking verb.

Helping verbs

Just as helpers in the world assist others, helping verbs assist the main verbs. Sometimes "to be" verbs function as helpers. Other helpers are

> *do, does, did, had, have, had, may, might, must, should, would, could, shall, will, can, ought, ought to, used to, need.*

While these helpers create a verb phrase, they do not follow the same grammatical rules as main verbs, which is why they are in a separate category.

Helping verbs, sometimes called *auxiliary* verbs, can be used before the word *not* whereas main verbs cannot. We say:

> *I might not go.*

But we do not say:

> *I saw not it.*

Another grammatical rule that doesn't apply to helping verbs is with contractions.

The *n't* can be attached to most helping verbs but never to main verbs. We say *can't* and *won't* but not *jumpn't* or *walkn't* (although children when they overlearn the rule sometimes do just that).

Helpers can be used before the subject to ask a question, but this is not possible with main verbs. We say:

> *Have you gone home?*

We do not say:

> *Gone you have home?*

• Remember:

Can means to be able; *may* means to have permission.

We sometimes get into usage problems with the helpers. *Had of* should never replace *had; had ought* and *should of* are considered illiterate; *have got* is either colloquial or redundant.

> Marty *can* do algebra.

> *May* I also tackle that algebra problem?

Transitive and intransitive verbs

For some reason lots of folks have trouble with transitive and intransitive verbs, so let's make this simple. *Transitus* comes from the Latin "to cross over." Verbs are transitive when the action of the "doer" crosses over the verb to the direct object.

> The dog *enjoys* the bone.

In this sentence *enjoys* is a transitive verb because the action of the dog "crosses over" the verb to *bone* the object.

The prefix *in-* means *not*—not *transitus*. So intransitive verbs do not cross over the verb; they do not take objects.

> The dogs *wait*.

In this sentence the verb is intransitive because nothing crosses over the verb from the subject *dogs*. It has no direct object.

Verb forms

Verb forms, sometimes called the "principal parts of the verb," are not to be confused with verb tenses. We use verb forms to **create** the tenses. For most verbs, there are five verb forms:

> the base verb, simple past, present participle, past participle, simple present third person singular.

Regular verbs

Regular verbs have five consistent forms; hence we describe them as *regular*.

> base—*work*
> simple past—*worked*
> present participle—*working*
> past participle—*worked*
> simple present third person singular, sometimes
> called the *-s* form—*works*

Regular verbs present no problem because the simple past and past participle are *always* formed the same way—by adding the suffixes *-ed* or *-d* to the base. No problem with the present participle and the simple present third person singular either because they *never change*. Adding the suffix *-ing* to the base forms the present participle, and adding *-s* or *-es* to the base forms the simple present.

These forms become so ingrained that primary or ELL students often overgeneralize the rules even for irregular verbs, saying things like:

> The dog *eated* the food.

Irregular verbs

Now we get to the sticky wicket—irregular verbs. They are called *irregular* because they are not consistent, especially in the simple past or the past participle. For example, we see this change with the irregular verb *eat*:

base—*eat*
simple past—*ate*
present participle—*eating*
past participle—*eaten*
third person singular—*eats*

Following are some other irregular verbs:

base	past tense	past participle
arise	arose	arisen
bear (carry/give birth)	bore	borne
begin	began	begun
blow	blew	blown
break	broke	broken
burst	burst	burst
choose	chose	chosen
dive	dived, dove	dived, dove
do	did	done
dream	dreamed, dreamt	dreamed, dreamt
drink	drank	drunk
eat	ate	eaten

get	got	got, gotten
know	knew	known
lay (place)	laid	laid
lie (recline)	lay	lain
ride	rode	ridden
run	ran	run
see	saw	seen
shake	shook	shaken
shine	shone, shined	shone, shined
shrink	shrank, shrunk	shrunk
sing	sang, sung	sung
speak	spoke	spoken
spring	sprang, sprung	sprung
steal	stole	stolen
swim	swam, swum	swum
take	took	taken
throw	threw	thrown
wake	waked, woke	waked, woke
wear	wore	worn
wring	wrung	wrung
write	wrote	written

Because these irregulars change in weird and wonderful ways, either memorize them or have a good, handy reference that lists them.

The lie/lay problem

Lie and *lay* are the most vexing irregular verbs of all. Let's get a handle on these vixens once and for all.

The irregular verb *lie* only has four principal parts or forms:

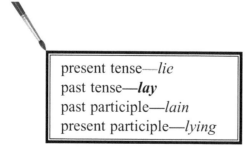

present tense—*lie*
past tense—***lay***
past participle—*lain*
present participle—*lying*

The irregular verb *lay* also only has four principal parts or forms:

> present tense—***lay***
> past tense—*laid*
> past participle—*laid*
> present participle—*laying*

See the problem? The past tense of *lie* is *lay,* which confuses it with the present tense of *lay.* Let's see if we can come up with some way to keep these verbs straight so we use them correctly.

Definition people find this helpful:

> *lie* means to recline whereas *lay* means to put something down.

Context people find this helpful:

> *lie* means the subject is doing something to himself or herself. *Lay* means that the subject is doing something to something or someone else.

Grammarians find this helpful:

> *lie* is intransitive and never takes a direct object, but *lay* is transitive and takes a direct object.

Still fuzzy? Someone once told us about this chart stratagem—and it is a gem. This works especially well for the visual learner. Try it. Memorize this simple chart. When asked for the correct word, either mentally reconstruct the chart or jot it down. This will help in writing and on tests.

subject to self	recline	**lie**	lay	lain	lying	no direct object
subject to others	put down	**lay**	laid	laid	laying	takes a direct object

Apply the chart to these sentences:

---

1. He lain/laid the books on the desk last week.
2. Yesterday afternoon she lay/laid down for a nap.
3. Lay/Lie the test on the table.
4. Last night I lay/laid the baby in her crib.
5. I will lie/lay down after I lie/lay the envelope on his desk.
6. Mother had lain/laid on her back all night.

Answers:

---

1. *Laid* is the correct answer because the subject is doing something to something else; it means to put down, and its direct object is *books.*
2. *Lay* is the correct answer because the subject is doing something to self; it means to recline, and there is no direct object, only an object of the preposition *nap.*
3. *Lay* is the correct answer because the subject (*you understood*) is doing something to something else; it means to put down, and the direct object is *test.*
4. *Laid* is the correct answer because the subject is doing something to someone else; *baby* is the direct object.
5. *Lie* is the correct answer because the subject is doing something to self; there is no direct object. *Lay* is the correct answer because the subject is doing something to something else and there is a direct object.
6. *Lain* is the correct answer because *lain* is the past participle form of *lie* and there is no direct object.

Once all eight possibilities are *laid* out within the context of subject, definition, and object, the logic becomes easy.

Verb Tenses

Simple tenses: Present, past, future

In Middle English the word *tens* or *tense* means *time* and that is what verb tenses tell us—the time. The easiest, or "simple," times are present, past, future.

Simple present tense

Something is happening or is existing right now.

> Watch how *he eats* his dinner.

Simple past tense

Something happened or existed before now.

> Last night *he ate* all his vegetables.

Simple future tense

Something will happen or come into existence after now.

> The doctor said *he will eat* better after the medicine.

Perfect tenses: Present perfect, past perfect, future perfect

A bit more complicated grammatically, the perfect tense is formed by *have, has, had, shall/will* plus the past participle.

Present perfect tense

Something started in the past with a connection to the present.

> They *have eaten lunch* so don't ask them to eat again.

In this sentence *they* started eating in the past but the connection is with not asking *them* to eat again now.

Past perfect tense

Something completed in the past, further back in time than other past actions; it is actually the past/past, indicating one past action happened before another past action. In other words, past perfect tense indicates the first of two past actions.

> He *had eaten* before he went to the picnic.

In this sentence, he ate and then went to the picnic. The word *had* clues us to which past action happened first.

Carroll had a student come for a writing conference. She read a sentence, *My grandmother had died* and asked this question: "Is the tense correct?"

Carroll responded, "I don't know."

The student repeated her question, apparently thinking Carroll had not heard the question. Carroll repeated, "I don't know."

The incredulous student stared. Finally, she asked, "Why not?"

Carroll went to the board and wrote *had died.* She circled *had.* "This is a signal word. It tells the reader that the action of the accompanying verb took place further back in time than the past action in the narrative. Since I don't know when your grandmother died in relation to the rest of the story, I can't help you out on tense."

Frustrated, the student exclaimed, "Is this why I memorized *has, had, have?*"

The story has a happy ending. After thinking about the signal word and the sentence, she announced, "It's had."

"Why is this so important to you?"

"I am going home for Thanksgiving when the family gathers and shares. I want to share this story, but it's got to be right."

Future perfect tense

Something that will happen in the future before another action in the future; it is actually the future/future, indicating one future action that will happen before another future action. In other words, the future perfect tense indicates the first of two future actions. It is formed with *shall* or *will have* and the past participle of the verb.

> He *will have eaten* before he goes home.

In this sentence the first future action is the eating; the second future action is going home.

Progressive tenses: Present progressive, past progressive, future progressive

Next, we have the progressive tense, which is formed by the verb *to be, will/shall*, and the present participle.

Present progressive tense

Some action is in progress in the now.

> He *is eating* his dinner.

Past progressive tense

Some action was in progress in the past.

> He *was eating* at Sandy's yesterday.

Future progressive tense

Some action will be in progress in the future.

> He *will be eating* with his mother tomorrow.

Perfect progressive tenses: Present perfect progressive, past perfect progressive, future perfect progressive

Combining the perfect and the progressive, gives us more tenses. The perfect progressive tense is formed by *has, had, have*, some form of *to be, shall/will*, and the present participle.

Present perfect progressive tense

Some continuous action that has been finished at some point in the past or continues to happen.

> He *has been eating* all day.

In this sentence the continuous act of eating happened all day.

Past perfect progressive tense

Some continuous action completed at some point in the past.

> He *had been eating* before the bell rang.

In this sentence the idea is he was eating but stopped when the bell rang.

Future perfect progressive tense

Some continuous action that will be completed at some time in the future. This tense is formed with *will, have,* and a "to be" verb.

> He *will have been eating* his lunch for thirty minutes by the time his friends come.

In this sentence he is eating but will stop when the friends arrive.

Teaching Tenses

When Wilson taught verb tenses, he came up with a stunning yet simple way to help kids remember how all these complicated tenses worked. He gave students long strips of paper—sentence strips, cash register tape, or regular paper taped together will do. They folded the strip in half. That crease was marked NOW. Everything to the left of NOW went into the PAST; everything to the right of

NOW went into the future. Then he directly taught the tenses. The students worked the tenses into the strips. Some used different colors; others used arrows; many relied on placement. Most told him they finally "got it."

The tense strip allowed students to see that tenses do not function in isolation. The context clarified the time of the tenses, and the timeline visual helped students internalize the concepts.

The tense time line

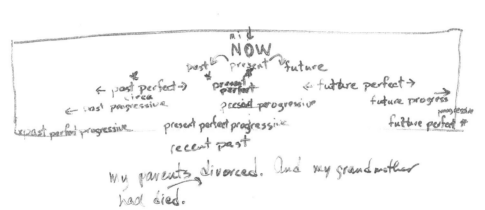

fig. 5.1

Verb Voice

Voice is one of many multi-meaning words. *Voice* may refer to the sound coming out of our mouths, the quality of someone's singing, the expression of choice, the writing style of an author, an idiolect, a speaker or a publication, even language itself. But *voice* in grammar—also called *diathesis*—when applied to verbs refers to the *active* and *passive*. That definition of *voice* often confuses people.

As with so much in language, the concept of *voice* evolved from Latin and Greek rhetoric. If we analyze *diathesis* from its Latin origins we see that the prefix *dia-* means "made of" or "consisting of" and the root *thesis* means "a statement." So when *voice* pertains to verbs, it literally means, "making a statement." Because

• Remember:

Telling students not to change their tenses is just flat out wrong. More accurately, everyone should check to make sure the tense they are using is in the right time period for what is said or written.

we make active and direct statements or passive and indirect statements, we end up with the terms *active* and *passive* voice.

In grammar, when the subjects do something to someone or something, we call it the *active voice*. When subjects have something done to them, we call it the *passive voice*. A helping verb, usually a "to be" verb, and the past participle of the verb grammatically form the passive voice. Some people ignore the verb construction as the key to the passive voice and say: "to form the passive move the subject part of the sentence to the predicate part." While generally weaker and wordier, we choose the passive voice when the receiver of the action is more important than the doer, when the doer is unknown, unimportant, or perhaps too obvious to mention, or to conceal the doer.

> The *gardener grew* the *roses.*

In this sentence the *gardener* (subject) is the doer who *grew* (verb) the *roses* (object), so we have the active voice.

> The *roses* (subject) *were grown* (verb) by the gardener.

In this sentence the *roses* (subject) had something done to them *were grown* (verb) by *the gardener* (object of the preposition).

The second sentence holds two more words than the first sentence, so in writing, we use the active voice for tighter construction.

Moody Verbs

We have a moody friend. Sometimes she is frank, stating things or asking questions. Other times she is demanding. But she is really a mess when she doubts us or wants things to be the way she thinks they should be.

Verbs are moody, too. Like our friend, they are all attitude. They want everyone to know the disposition of the subject toward the action. And, like our friend, they have three moods: the indicative, the imperative, and the subjunctive.

The indicative mood

The indicative mood states facts, opinions, or asks questions.

> I think grammar reinforces good writing.

I *indicate* how I feel about grammar. I just say it.

The imperative mood

The imperative mood commands, demands, or requests.

> Boys and girls, please complete the grammar exercises on page ten for homework.

I am issuing a request that is *imperative* or urgent.

The subjunctive mood

We write conditional sentences in the subjunctive mood to convey doubt, desire, or something supposed. When using the subjunctive, everything is up for grabs because one part expresses a truth that is unverified (the *would of, could of, should of* clause).

> If she gets off early from work, she could come to the party.

In the hypothetical or contrary-to-fact conditional, we follow a wish or an implied wish with the verb *were.*

> I wish I *were* a millionaire so I could give millions to charity. (stated wish)

> If I *were* a millionaire, I would give generously to charities. (implied wish)

As with other formalities such as *who/whom,* for example, many writers honor the "wish/were" rule, but others just use the indicative *was.*

> If I *was* a millionaire . . .

Verbals

Piggybacking on verbs are verbals—but be clear, they are **not** verbs, they just resemble verbs and that gets everyone in trouble, especially on tests. People often mistake verbals for verbs. But, here comes that word again, verbals serve a different *function* than do verbs. The three verbals are infinitives, gerunds, and participles.

Infinitives

We form the infinitive with *to* plus the base form of a verb—*to work.* Usually infinitives function as nouns, but sometimes they are adjectives or adverbs.

> *To work* is satisfying.

Here *to work* functions as a noun and the subject of the sentence.

> I love *to work.*

Here *to work* functions as a noun and the object of *love.*

> He got an idea *to work.*

Here *to work* functions as an adjective modifying *idea* although we'd probably say "a working idea."

> The boss repeatedly reminded her *to work.*

Here *to work* functions as an adverb modifying *repeatedly reminded*. Ah! the joys of English grammar.

Gerunds

Gerunds look like verbs but work like nouns. They end in *-ing* and function as nouns, but not all words that end in *-ing* are gerunds—they could be present participles.

> *Working* is satisfying.

In this sentence *working* is a noun and the subject of the sentence.

> Rosario liked *working*.

In this sentence *working* is a noun; object of liked.

Participles

Participles are verbals that also end in *-ing* for present participle, or *-ed, -d, -t, -en, -n* for the past participle. Participles usually function as adjectives; think of them as verbal adjectives.

> The *working* mother had little time to rest.

Here *working* is a participle functioning as an adjective by modifying *mother*.

> *Sulking*, the boy pouted all day in school.

Here *sulking* is the participle—verbal adjective—modifying *the boy*.

> Lisa, *noticing her sister*, crossed the street to meet her.

Noticing her sister is the participial phrase modifying *Lisa*.

To + a verb = an infinitive
To travel proves educational.

to + a noun = a prepositional phrase
Mary went *to the house*.

Gerunds always function as nouns.

Participial phrases function the same way as adjectives—both modify nouns.

Remember:

To avoid the dreaded "dangling participle," place the participial phrase as close as possible to the noun it modifies. If you don't, the results may confuse, be misunderstood, or may be downright funny. These results may negatively affect a piece of writing. So take this hint: if there is a participial phrase in a sentence, underline the noun closest to it. Then make sure the noun and phrase make sense together.

> *Changing the oil every 5,000 miles*, the car ran better.

In this sentence the car did not change the oil. It needs a rewrite.

> *Changing the oil every 5,000 miles,* the mechanic increased the car's gas mileage.

Revised, the sentence clearly states that the mechanic did the oil change.

> *Hitting the ball in the air*, the bat fell on the ground.

While the bat may have hit the ball, it is unlikely it did so without a person holding it. This sentence lacks the logic of cause and effect and needs to be revised.

> *Hitting the ball in the air,* the batter dropped the bat on the ground and ran to first base.

Remember:

When catching such errors, the writer enhances the piece with more specific language and better writing.

EVERYTHING ELSE:

PREPOSITIONS, CONJUNCTIONS, INTERJECTIONS

> "From now on, ending a sentence with a preposition is something up with which I shall not put."
> —attributed to Winston Churchill

Prepositions

Prepositions, small but important words, show the relationship of a noun, pronoun, or noun equivalent to another part of a sentence. That is why we call prepositions *function* words. In Latin and Old English, there were no prepositions—all relationships were conveyed through endings—and there were lots more of them than we have in modern English. Now we have the *'s* ending to show possession; *s* or *es* to show the plural.

In Old English we would have written *pæm scipum* with a dative case ending on both words to mean "to the ships." By the time the language evolved into Middle English, endings were dropped and the preposition was born, so we wrote "*to the shippes.*" Middle English used the preposition and the common plural ending, as does our modern English "*to the ships.*"

Think about it—the word *preposition* literally means *pre* (before) *position* (the right place), so prepositions are little words that are pre positioned. They "go before" the noun to show its relationship to other words in the sentence. Neat, huh?

Prepositional phrases

We form prepositional phrases by adding a preposition (simple or phrasal) before a noun, pronoun, or noun equivalent.

> The boat moved *toward the wharf.*

Toward is the preposition; *the wharf* is its object.

Common prepositions
about, above, across, after, against, along, among, around, at,
before, behind, below, beneath (under), beside (by, near), besides (as well, also, further)
between, beyond, but, by,
concerning,
despite, during, down, expecting, for, from, in, inside, into,
like,
near,
of, off, on, onto, out, outside, over,
regarding, round,
past,
since,
through, throughout, till, to, toward,
until, under, underneath (beneath), up, upon,
with, within, without

Phrasal prepositions

Phrasal prepositions function as one preposition but consist of more than one word. They are the prepositional part of a prepositional phrase, so don't confuse phrasal prepositions with prepositional phrases.

Phrasal prepositions:

> *in front of; according to*

Both of these phrases function as one preposition.

> George stands *in front of* Stacy *according to* the teacher's list.

Stacy is the object of the prepositional phrase *in front of.*

> *According to the teacher,* we all did well on the test.

According to acts as one preposition; *the teacher* is its object.

> *Because of* her assignment, she sat *in front of* the bookcase.

Because of is the phrasal preposition used as one preposition with *her assignment* as the noun, the object of the preposition; *in front of* is the phrasal preposition used as one preposition with *the bookcase* as the noun, the object of the preposition. Thus, phrasal prepositions act exactly like a single preposition in creating a prepositional phrase.

• Remember:

A preposition *always* pre-positions a noun, pronoun, or noun equivalent: *to the garden, by the wall, over the street.*

When you have the word *to* and a verb, you have the verbal *infinitive* not a prepositional phrase: *to go, to run, to wish.*

Common phrasal prepositions
according to, along with, apart from, as for, as regards, as to, as of, as far as, because of, by means of, by reason of, by way of, due to, except for, in addition to, in case of, in front of, in lieu of, in view of, in place of, in regard to, in spite of, instead of, on account of, next to, out of, owing to, up to, with regard to, with respect to, with reference to, with the exception of

• Remember:

A phrasal
preposition is
used as if it were
just one
preposition.

Some thoughts on *up*

Prepositions can be misunderstood sometimes, so we always have to remember to consider their function. Take the two-letter word *up*. If *up* means toward the sky or at the top of the list, why do we wake *up*? We warm *up* leftovers yet clean *up* the kitchen. We lock *up* the house and fix *up* our cars. How about stirring *up* trouble, lining *up* for tickets, or working *up* an appetite? Worse: a drain must be opened *up* because it's stopped *up*. We open *up* a store in the morning, but we close it *up* at night. Actually, if you look *up* up in a dictionary, it has about thirty definitions.

To bollix up *up* further, Pixar has a 2009 children's movie entitled *Up*. That, of course, would make *Up* a proper noun. You just gotta' love English!

Ruthie is up to her "teaching" again. This time she tackles "PREPS." James, who seems to have lost interest in these lessons, interrupts to Ruthie's consternation, proving C.S. Peirce's theory of abductive reasoning is alive and well in kids.

fig. 6.1 By permission of Rick Detorie and Creators Syndicate, Inc.

Conjunctions

The word *conjunction* comes from the Latin and Greek prefix *con-* meaning *with* and the root *junct,* which means *to join.* That's exactly what conjunctions do; they join words, phrases, clauses, and sentences. They are joiners.

Coordinating conjunctions

Like *co*-workers who are equal, these conjunctions join equal parts in sentences—words, phrases, or clauses. There are only seven and are often called by their mnemonic device

F A N B O Y S—*for, and, nor, but, or, yet, so.*

Mary *and* Helen attended the concert.

And connects the equal parts of the compound subject.

Mary attended the concert *and* the party.

And connects the equal parts of the compound predicate.

Mary attended the concert, *but* Helen went to the party.

Here *but* connects two equal independent clauses.

The functions of *and*

Poor *and* gets taken for granted, yet *and* serves the language well and often. Actually there are sixteen different functions for *and*.

1. to express a connection

I like to ride the Ferris wheel *and* the bumper cars at the carnival.

Note: *Ferris* is capitalized because George Washington Gale Ferris, an American engineer, designed the wheel that would carry passengers for the World's Columbian Exposition 1893, in Chicago, Illinois.

2. to link word with word

> Eat your bread *and* butter.

3. to link phrase with phrase

> I love the Thanksgiving song "Over the River *and* through the Woods."

4. to convey a combination

> She is smart *and* likely to take advantage of a substitute teacher.

5. to "fill in" as an expletive

> *And* it came to pass.

6. to repeat

> She read the story over *and* over *and* over again.

7. to vary

> The music played soft *and* slow *and* then fast *and* furious.

8. to convey logical movement

> First came job losses, *and* money became tight, *and* then stress hit the workers.

9. to join two adjectives

> The blanket was nice *and* warm.

10. to join two verbs

> Maria planned *and* executed the arrangements for the party.

11. to join two verbs, when one states a position while the other shows action

> Jacob sat *and* ate his oatmeal.

12. to show a consequence and sequel

> The principal ordered, "Go," *and* the teacher went.

13. to show contrary action

> We promised to respond *and* didn't.

14. to refer to alternatives

> You have to choose between him *and* me.

● Remember:

Even small words
like conjunctions
have many
functions in
English.

15. to provide a supplementary explanation

> He *and* he alone can do the job.

16. to show a point of junction

> Meet me at the corner of Main *and* First.

Subordinating conjunctions

*Sub*ways and *sub*marines are "beneath" or "under" the ground or water. *Sub*ordinating conjunctions are also "beneath" or "under" in the sense that they signal a clause of lesser importance. They join *un*equal parts in sentences. They introduce a part of the sentence, called a dependent or subordinate clause, which holds a lesser meaning or enjoys a lesser status. The following mnemonic device helps us remember the most common subordinating conjunctions:

3 A's	AAA	*after, although, as*
2 B's	BB	*because, before*
tu tu	TUTU	*though, unless/than, until*
is	IS	*if, since*
6 W's	WWWWWW	*when, whenever, while, where, wherever, whether*

Notice the use of the subordinating conjunction *before* in the following sentence:

> *Before* José blows the debris into neat piles, he mows the lawn.

Clearly the important or main clause in this sentence is that *José mows the lawn*. That *he blows the debris into neat piles* is of less importance because that action is dependent on the mowing happening first; therefore, the subordinate or dependent clause is introduced with the subordinate conjunction *before*.

• Remember:

A *subordinating* conjunction, signals a clause that is of less importance.

The then/than problem

Then is an adverb that refers to time; *than* is a conjunction used in comparisons.

> When mixing the dogs' food, first put in the kibbles, and *then* add the water.

In this sentence *then* helps the reader know the time sequence of preparing the dogs' food.

> Chanel runs faster *than* Coco, but Coco jumps higher *than* Chanel.

This sentence uses *than* to compare Chanel and Coco as they run and jump.

Correlative conjunctions

Think of correlative conjunctions as "co-related." They are two words acting like a brother and sister, husband and wife, yin and yang. Corrclatives are pairs of related words. These pairs are indispensable for linking grammatically equal elements and for writing sound parallel constructions.

> both . . . and
> not only . . . but also
> not . . . but
> either . . . or neither . . . nor
> whether . . . or
> as . . . as

Jo wrote *both* an essay *and* a poem.

Both . . . and show the relationship of what Jo wrote; therefore, *essay* and *poem* are grammatically linked.

Peter sunk *not only* one basket in the first quarter *but also* five baskets in the second quarter.

This sentence illustrates nice parallel structure: *one basket/ in the/first quarter—five baskets/in the/second quarter.*

Either you go with me *or* I'll go alone.

Either . . . or show related alternatives: *you go with me/ I'll go alone.*

Conjunctive adverbs

Conjunctive adverbs join two clauses. The most common conjunctive adverbs are

accordingly, again, also, besides consequently, finally, furthermore, however, indeed, more-over, nevertheless, otherwise, then, therefore, and thus.

I taught every grade level; *however*, I most enjoyed teaching high school.

She recited the stanza perfectly. *Indeed*, she recited the entire poem perfectly.

The like/as problem

The like or as problem presents the perfect case to support why knowing the parts of speech helps correctness. *Like* is a preposition; *as* is a conjunction. Why does knowing that make a difference? Here's why.

Nouns and pronouns follow the preposition *like* thereby forming a prepositional phrase.

> Addy looks like her mother; Von looks like his father.

In this sentence the noun *mother* follows the first *like*; *father* follows the second *like*. Both *mother* and *father* are objects of the preposition *like*.

Clauses follow the conjunction *as*.

> The crowd on the beach laughed *as* the wave broke over the surfers.

The clause *the wave broke over the surfers* follows *as*. The subject is *wave*; the verb is *broke*.

Like is never used with clauses—at least not in standard English. Although students today often do just that in colloquial kids speak.

> *Like* he is something else!

Sometimes the word *like* is used as a verb.

> Eddie *likes* his steaks medium rare.

In this sentence *likes* is a verb indicating a taste for his meat cooked a certain way.

Like may also be used to compare.

> Our family proves the old adage "*like* father, *like* son."

With metaphors and similes, the rule holds.

> I am a frisky puppy today.

The metaphor of calling myself a *frisky puppy* is clear.

> I am frisky like a puppy today.

The simile *like a puppy* is grammatically correct.

> I am as frisky *as* a puppy playing with a ball.

• Remember:

A noun or
pronoun follows
like; a subject and
verb follow *as*.

Now the simile demands a subject and verb following that *as*. (The first *as* is an adverb showing the same extent or degree.)

Starting Sentences with *and* or *but*

Once and we wish for all—it is fine to begin sentences with *and* or *but*. Just don't overdo it. There is no grammatical reason that prohibits starting a sentence with *and* or *but*. People who insist upon it are misinformed and lack grammatical understanding. This notion, born of myth not correctness, continues to bedevil us. Robert Lowth stated it was perfectly "fine" to start a sentence with *and* or *but*. We would like to think the matter settled since Lowth addressed it in 1762, yet here we are almost 250 years later with people still believing the myth.

Interjections

Interjections are the fun words because they show surprise or some emotion: *Wow! Hooray! Right On! Congrats! Cool! Man! Ouch!* That's it. An exclamation point, comma, or dash follows the interjection. If we use a comma, we place the exclamation point at the end of the exclamatory sentence.

Teaching Parts of Speech

Challenge students by inviting them to make a circular book. It's fun and accommodates eight parts. Students will need card stock, Scotch tape, pencils and washable colored markers with fine points.

Making the book

- Trace two equal circles at least ten inches in diameter on card stock and cut them out. (Inexpensive paper plates may be used but must be flattened.)
- Fold the circles in half one way and then fold them in half the other way to create four sections or four pieces of "pie."
- With the circles on top of each other cut along one crease from the outside of the circle to the center, the mid-point.
- Number each section lightly in pencil—the top circle pieces 1, 2, 3, 4; the bottom circle pieces 5, 6, 7, 8. (The number 1 piece of the top circle should rest on top of the number 5 piece of the bottom circle.)
- Flip up the number 1 piece so the piece numbered 5 shows.
- Tape piece 4 to piece 5; it is best to tape underneath to maximize writing space.
- Now the circular book is ready. (see fig. 6.2)
- Fold piece 1 so it rests on piece 2; fold both 1 and 2 over on top of section 3; fold 1, 2, and 3 on top of piece 4; fold 1, 2, 3, and 4 on top of 5; fold 1, 2, 3, 4, and 5 on top of 6; fold 1, 2, 3, 4, 5, and 6 on top of 7; fold 1, 2, 3, 4, 5, 6, and 7 on top of 8. The book is compact and may be kept easily in a writer's notebook. (see fig. 6.3)

The eight parts of speech

As you teach and model each part of speech, students follow the model and fill in the pieces of the "pie." CAUTION:

This is not a one-day strategy. Most teachers take a week on each part of speech (in addition to teaching other aspects of the curriculum), allowing students to use and identify the part of speech in their writing, studying mentor texts, and learning all the nuances surrounding a particular part of speech. Just memorizing the definition will not work; students must be able to analyze the function. This is a good way to integrate grammar, literature and reading, and writing. These may be displayed or folded back into sections and placed in their writer's notebook as a handy reference.

- In each section, students, following the model, write the name of the part of speech in the narrow section of the "pie," the definition in their own words, plus examples, exceptions, forms, and so forth. (see fig. 6.4)
- On the back of the "piece of pie" students find examples in their own writing and in a book they are reading. Following is one slice of "pie" done by a fourth-grade student.

nouns

these name everything

China, Susan, horse, love, ladybug, gang

most nouns make the plural with S but some add ES,
so watch out

In my reading: *Maybe Yes, Maybe No, Maybe, Maybe* by Susan Patron, I found lots of nouns. I picked page 30: story, Rabbit (girl's nickname), Rebecca, PK, Rabba, baby, people, name, pie, Mama.

In my writing: I use lots of nouns. Here are some from chapter one "In the Beginning" of my latest book <u>The Horse in the Cupboard</u>: horse, cupboard, name, Secratairiet [sic.], races, La Bahia Downs Stables, Mr. Harris, Bonnie, desk. (see fig. 6.5)

Teaching Idea

Circular Book

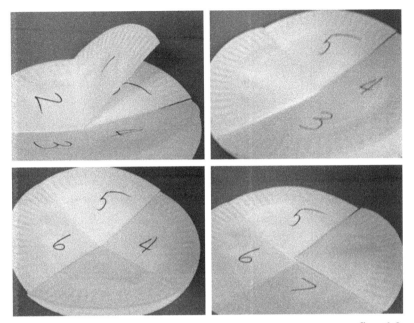

fig. 6.2

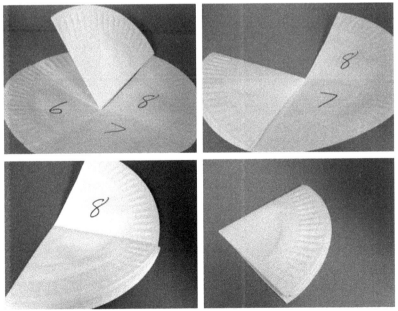

fig. 6.3

Teaching Idea

Parts of Speech in the Round

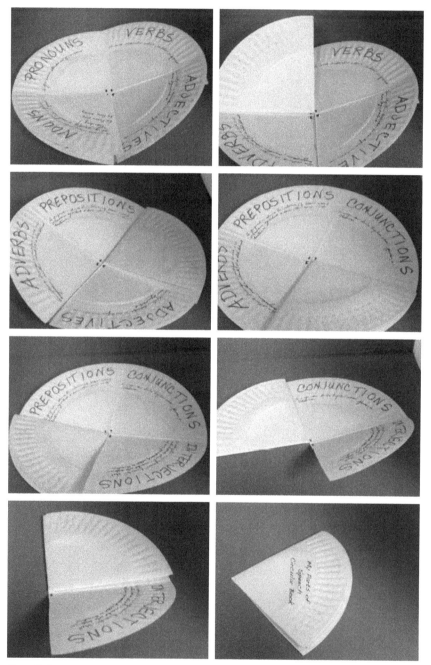

fig. 6.4

fig. 6.5

Extension of the circular book

It is easy to extend these books by adding more sections, but most teachers invite the students to make additional books out of specific parts of speech. For example, keeping in mind that writing is a mode of learning, students may make a book of pronouns with the eight parts being: personal, reflexive and intensive, demonstrative, relative, interrogative, indefinite, reciprocal, and possessive. They may make verb circular books or adjective circular books, and so forth. These are festive and colorful when displayed in the classroom.

PARTS AND PARCELS:

PHRASES AND CLAUSES

> "Exalted ideas of fancy require to be clothed in a suitable vesture of phrase."
> —Aristophanes

Phrases

We wish there were some way to jazz up phrases, but in truth, to para*phrase*—no pun intended—Gertrude Stein, a phrase is a phrase is a phrase in English grammar. Simply defined, a phrase is a group of related words without a subject or predicate.

Phrases come in several varieties: noun, appositive, gerund, infinitive, participial, verb, adverbial, adjectival, prepositional, and absolute.

Knowing the parts of speech helps identify each.

Noun phrases

In Africa the saying goes,

> "*Kushayw'edonsayo.*" (Zulu).
>
> "The lead cow (the one in front) gets whipped the most."

When plowing fields, farmers choose a lead cow. Out in front, she makes sure the others follow her so everything is done just right. The farmers carefully watch her; if anything goes wrong, she gets the whipping.

This Zulu axiom captures the notion that whoever does the most difficult job gets blamed for everything that goes wrong, so the leader gets the pressure. That sums up the noun phrase. If there is no lead noun in a phrase, there is no noun phrase. That lead noun signals a noun phrase and takes all the pressure off all its modifiers, which can include other phrases such as prepositional phrases.

> *The elderly couple in the park* feed the squirrels every day.

Here *couple* is the lead noun; *the* is the definite article that refers to *couple, elderly* is the adjective modifying *couple,* and *in the park* is the prepositional phrase that further modifies *the elderly couple.*

Appositive phrases

Remember those two second-grade "appositives" girl-friends in the noun section? They're back! This time they brought along a few more words. Like a noun in apposition, an appositive phrase renames the noun it follows. Appositives are helpful phrases to clarify or amplify relationships, sites, times, and other details.

> While writing this book, we shared chapters as we wrote them with Sharon, *our patient editor.*

The appositive phrase is *our patient editor* as it renames the proper noun *Sharon.*

Infinitive phrases

We know what forms an infinitive from the "Verbals" section: *to* + *verb*. That's half the battle because an infinitive phrase just adds an object. So it is *to* + *verb* + *the object of the infinitive* and other words that are part of the phrase. As a unit, they act as nouns, adjectives, or adverbs.

> I love *to cook chiles rellenos.*

In this sentence *to cook* is the infinitive with *chiles rellenos* as its object, so the entire phrase *to cook chiles rellenos* functions as a noun, the direct object of the verb *love*.

If, however, we write

> I don't have the time *to cook chiles rellenos.*

to cook chiles rellenos acts as an adjective phrase modifying the noun *time.*

If we write

> I was invited *to cook chiles rellenos.*

to cook chiles rellenos turns adverbial because it modifies the verb phrase *was invited* by telling us why we were invited.

Gerund phrases

Since gerunds are verbals ending in *-ing*, and since they act as nouns, gerund phrases function as units that can do anything a noun can do. They can be subjects, complements, direct objects, or objects of prepositions. Let's look at a few.

> *Studying for tests* is a good thing to do.

In this sentence *Studying for tests* is the gerund phrase acting as the subject.

> A disastrous habit for students is *goofing off before tests.*

● Remember:

Always check the function of the phrase, that is, how it is used in the context of the sentence.

In this sentence *goofing off before tests* is the gerund phrase used as a complement.

> Karina enjoyed *studying in the library with friends.*

Here *studying in the library with friends* shows the gerund phrase as object.

> Latisha is not interested in *studying calculus this semester.*

• Remember:

Studying calculus this semester, the gerund phrase, is the object of the preposition *in.*

Other phrases, especially prepositional phrases, are often part of the gerund phrase.

Participial phrases

The word *participle* comes from the same Latin word *participialis* that gives us words such as: *participate, participant, participation, participator, participative, participatory*—all of which suggest a sharing or partaking. So logically participial phrases are also into the sharing business. Because they always function as adjectives, they share all the complements or modifiers of the noun.

Participial phrases are formed with the present participle *-ing,* or with the past participle *-ed* for regular verbs (they take other forms for irregular verbs) and all their complements and modifiers—hence these phrases function as adjectives.

> *Being an avid reader*, George tripped to the library twice a week.

This participial phrase beginning with the participle *being* shares *an avid reader,* so the entire phrase modifies *George.*

> Jessica, *working overtime at the factory,* got a raise.

This participial phrase beginning with the participle *working* shares *overtime at the factory,* so the entire phrase modifies *Jessica.*

> The theatre, *closed since late May*, will open in September.

• Remember:

Keep participial phrases near the noun they are modifying.

This participial phrase beginning with *closed* shares *since late May,* so the entire phrase modifies *theatre.*

Verb phrases

Think this is an easy one? Not so fast. There are two ways of looking at verb phrases. The first is the narrow definition: the main verb, helping verbs, and other infinitive or participle constructions.

> The seniors *were given* a rousing round of applause at graduation.

• Remember:

Looks are deceiving. While easy to spot a simple verb phrase, it is not always easy to tease out the meaning of all verb phrases.

Analyzing what is happening— the function— in the following sentence is key.

Here the verb phrase is simply the verb and its helper. *Were given* is the verb phrase.

But, and not to get too technical, in generative grammar (the grammar based on Noam Chomsky's theories) a verb phrase may consist of the main verb (the simple predicate), helping verbs, plus what generative grammarians call *specifers,* that is short, frequently occurring function words, complements, and adjuncts—those words that express negation, time, place, manner, instrument, reason, purpose, condition, and degree. In other words the predicate and everything that explains it, becomes the verb phrase. (See more about predicates in chapter eight.)

> Bill *watched Ray play Little League baseball yesterday.*

So according to generative grammar, in this sentence the entire predicate is the verb phrase. After the main verb *watched,* the verb phrase contains a direct object and the adjuncts that express time, manner, instrument, and condition.

I *am leaving* next week is decidedly different than I *am leaving* now, yet the verb phrase *am leaving* is the same in both.

Adjectival phrases

• Remember:

Avoid words such as *very* and *really* if they don't carry their own weight.

Try for a more precise adjective. *Very sad* would be stronger if consolidated into *despondent* or *mournful*.

This is a good time to consult both a dictionary and a thesaurus.

Not to be confused with participial phrases that function as adjectives, usually adjectival phrases are simple combinations of an adjective and its preceding intensifier as in *very sad*. Adjectival phrases modify nouns or pronouns.

> Everyone was *heavyhearted and inconsolable* at the funeral.

Heavyhearted and inconsolable is the predicate adjective phrase modifying *everyone*.

> Fred ran with grace yet David, *not too clumsy*, won the race.

The adjectival phrase *not too clumsy* describes David.

> Is the refrigerator *cold enough*?

The adjectival phrase *cold enough* modifies the noun *refrigerator*.

> My father was *easy to please* on Father's Day.

Easy to please is the adjectival phrase that describes *father*.

• Remember:

An adjectival phrase is a single unit that acts as one gigantic adjective modifying a noun or noun phrase.

Adverbial phrases

Even if we are not techies, most of us know that there are two types of operating software: "systems," which is quick and easy, and "applications" that allows for people to do more. Adverbial phrases are like operating software; they come in two types. One is quick and easy, simply a short expression that intensifies as it modifies; the other allows more wiggle room, any phrase or combination of phrases, usually prepositional that acts like an adverb when it modifies.

> Joshua writes *creatively but slowly.*

Here *creatively but slowly* is the "systems" adverbial phrase. It's quick and easy—two adverbs strung together with *but.*

> Sally, the librarian, said she would meet the students *before the holiday recess.*

Here *before the holiday recess* is the "applications" adverbial phrase. It allows a prepositional phrase to wiggle in, but it functions as an adverbial phrase.

Prepositional phrases

The darling of English teachers, prepositional phrases are easiest to teach because they always begin with a preposition and end with a noun or noun equivalent that serves as the object. These phrases function as adjectives or adverbs.

• Remember:

Adverbial phrases modify every-thing except nouns and pronouns.

> Walter originally came *from Jersey City,* which is *in New Jersey.*

From and *in* introduce the two prepositional phrases in this sentence. *Jersey City,* the proper noun of the city and *New Jersey,* the proper noun of the state complete the phrases.

• Remember:

Prepositional phrases are different from phrasal prepositions.

Absolute phrases

Since there is so little absolute in grammar, it is refreshing to find something absolute. Absolute phrases, sometimes called the nominative absolute, are so named because they *absolutely* modify the main subject and verb; they add information. They generally consist of a noun or pronoun and a participle as well as any related modifiers.

> *His reputation as a shooter secured by his individual record,* Jackson readied for the NBA playoffs.

The entire introductory absolute phrase *His reputation as a shooter secured by his individual record* modifies the independent clause (see clauses) *Jackson readied for the NBA playoffs.*

> The two authors at the conference autographed their books all day, *their expressions beaming delightedly.*

The concluding phrase *their expressions beaming delightedly* modifies the entire preceding independent clause.

> *Everything considered,* the prom was a big success.

• Remember:

Something absolute is unconditional; absolute phrases modify the entire main clause within a sentence or sometimes the entire sentence.

Notice how *everything considered* adds additional information to the independent clause it modifies.

Phrases as fragments

Because some phrases can be long, because they often have a subject or verb (but never both) or verbal in them, it is easy to mistake them for complete sentences. Watch out for something like this:

> The teacher suddenly looked up from the book. *Her eyes twinkling with amusement.*

That verbal *twinkling*, a participle, tricks people into thinking they have a complete sentence.

This fragment may easily be fixed by changing the participle to a verb.

> Her eyes *twinkled* with amusement.

Phrases as dangling modifiers

Phrases that dangle are often due to misplacing the word to which the modifier refers, so the phrase just dangles away. Even folks who know better sometimes make this mistake.

> *Having moved at twelve,* her hometown was no longer familiar.

This sounds as if the hometown moved when it was twelve since *hometown* is closest to the phrase.

Try revising this dangling modifier so the sentence makes sense.

> *Having moved at twelve,* Mary found her hometown was no longer familiar.

Extraneous phrases

Called "deadwood" by some grammarians or "bad words" by others, extraneous phrases often clutter our speaking and writing.

Examples of extraneous phrases:
get in touch with
sort of
kind of
as far as . . . concerned
involved with
generally speaking
all things considered
something like
a little bit
due to the fact that
in many cases
the fact that
in many instances
type of

• Remember:

A phrase can be part of a clause, but a clause cannot be part of a phrase.

Be aware of these wasted words and revise.

Clauses

E very time we hear the word *clause,* we think of the exchange between Groucho and Chico Marx in the 1935 movie *A Night at the Opera.* Groucho attempts to explain a business contract to Chico, but Chico, as usual, misunderstands and thinks Groucho is trying to convince him there is a Santa Claus.

> Groucho: "That's in every contract; that's what you call a sanity clause."
>
> Chico: "You can't a fool me. There ain't no sanity clause."

It's a wonderful bit in the movie, but we wonder how many people end up feeling like Chico when they study clauses. So let's bring some sanity to clauses.

Clauses are like phrases because they are a group of related words, but clauses are also like sentences because they have a subject and a verb (predicate). Sometimes the only thing that distinguishes a clause from a sentence is terminal punctuation.

> Puppies play endlessly

This could be labeled a *main* or *independent clause.* It contains a subject and a predicate and no terminal mark. It stands ready for a dependent clause, a prepositional phrase, perhaps even an interjection, or that final punctuation mark.

> Puppies play endlessly!

When we add that terminal mark, we change the clause to an *exclamatory sentence.* It contains a subject and a predicate and terminal punctuation. As with most things in English, it all boils down to function.

Independent or main clauses

When kids leave home for college, they feel liberated. They want their independence. They want to make their own decisions, be their own bosses, and be self-reliant. They want to stand alone. So, too, when clauses go off into sentences, some want to be independent; they want to stand alone. We call these clauses *independent* because they stand alone. They make sense and do not need any help.

• Remember:

Many grammar books use the terms *independent clause* and *main clause* interchangeably.

> *The car rattled*

is one independent clause. Its subject, *car*; its verb, *rattled*. If it were followed by a terminal punctuation mark, it would be a sentence.

> The car rattled down the street and the windows shook in my office

Here we find two independent clauses: *car rattled* and *windows shook*. The entire first clause, including the prepositional phrase is *The car rattled down the street.* The entire second clause, including the prepositional phrase is *the windows shook in my office. And* is the coordinating conjunction joining the two clauses.

Restrictive and nonrestrictive clauses

We always had trouble remembering which is which with these two clauses, so to remember we often substitute *necessary* and *not necessary.*

Restrictive clauses

Restrictive or necessary clauses are essential to the meaning of the sentence.

> The lawnmower *that I bought last week* has already broken down.

that I bought last week is necessary in the sentence because it excludes, limits, or restricts the subject lawnmower from all other lawnmowers with the information *that I bought last week*.

Nonrestrictive clauses

Nonrestrictive or unnecessary clauses are not really essential to the meaning of the sentence. The information may be interesting, even important, or relevant, but not essential.

> The lawnmower, which has sharp blades, cut easily through the grass.

which has sharp blades is nonrestrictive or unnecessary to the meaning of that sentence; it is extraneous, unnecessary information. The point is the lawnmower cuts easily. We could infer it does so because the blades are sharp.

Dependent clauses

In the real world, we say people or things are dependent when they rely on someone or something else for support; they cannot stand alone. In each of the following sentences, someone or something is vulnerable and requires some aid for support to function or even to live.

• Remember:

Nonrestrictive clauses are set apart from the rest of the sentence with commas.

> My ninety-four-year-old mother *depended* on her "wheelie" to walk.
>   Without her "wheelie" my mother was unable to walk.

> Baby Doe was totally *dependent* upon others for survival.
>   If others did not care for Baby Doe, she would have died.

> Craig *depends* upon his car to get to work.
>   Without his car, Craig would be unable to work.

> That exotic plant *needs* certain fertilizer to grow.
>
> Exotic plants are dependent upon certain fertilizers, or they wither and die.

> Grass *won't grow* without water and sunlight.
>
> Grass depends upon water and photosynthesis to grow.

Dependency works exactly the same way in grammar. Dependent clauses need something else—an independent clause—in order to survive, work, or make sense. Dependent clauses come in two categories: relative and subordinate.

Relative clauses

Relative clauses are introduced by a relative pronoun that refers back to the noun or noun phrase it references in the independent clause. In grammar talk, this is called its *antecedent*, a terribly academic sounding word that comes from the Latin *antecedere* meaning "one who goes before." Relative clauses may be restrictive (necessary) or unrestrictive (unnecessary).

> Jason, *who wants a swimming pool*, swims every day at the gym.

In this sentence *who* is the relative pronoun introducing the relative unrestrictive clause (unnecessary) *who wants a swimming pool*. Its antecedent is *Jason*. The fact that Jason may want a swimming pool, while interesting and perhaps even motivational, is not necessary for the reader to understand that he swims every day at the gym. So that relative clause is unrestrictive.

> Andrew told me *that a polyp, which was in his colon,* had to be removed.

• Remember:

That may be a relative or demonstrative pronoun.

As a pronoun, *that* introduces a restrictive or necessary clause and is never preceded by a comma.

In this sentence we have two relative clauses—one restrictive and one unrestrictive. The first: *that a polyp* is a relative restrictive (necessary) clause introduced by the relative pronoun *that,* and the second: *which was in his colon* is a relative unrestrictive (unnecessary) clause introduced by the relative pronoun *which.* While the fact that the polyp is situated in his colon may be important, say to Andrew's doctor or surgeon, it is not necessary to know that grammatically to understand it had to be removed.

Subordinate clauses

As we have already established the prefix *sub* means below or under. A *sub*ordinate clause is below or under the independent (or main) clause in meaning. While it may be important, it simply is not *as* important as the information in the independent clause. Subordinate clauses are always introduced by a subordinate conjunction, and they function as adjectives, adverbs, or nouns.

> *While* I washed the dogs, the telephone rang.

Because *while* is a subordinate conjunction and because subordinate conjunctions introduce subordinate clauses, *While I washed the dogs* is less important than the fact that the telephone rang. Stated differently, *the telephone rang* is the main idea or independent clause in that sentence.

We further subdivide the dependent subordinate and relative clauses into adverb, adjective, and noun clauses.

Adverb clauses

Adverb clauses are subordinate clauses that modify verbs, adjectives, adverbs, or the main clause. Like adverbs themselves, adverb clauses tell the where, when, how, or why about the main clause, expressing time, place, direction, cause, effect, condition, manner, or concession.

> *When the movie is over*, we will grab a hamburger.

• Remember:

Subordinate (dependent) clauses are not as important as main (independent) clauses.

When the movie is over is the adverb clause telling when the hamburger event will happen. When it comes first in the sentence, a comma separates it from the main or independent clause.

It is also possible to flip flop the sentence, but no comma is needed.

> We will grab a hamburger when the movie is over.

> *Because her alarm clock didn't ring,* she was late for school.

This entire clause modifies the main clause *she was late for school. Because* signals a cause and effect relationship.

The Because/Since Problem

Some folks incorrectly use *because* and *since* interchangeably; some just misuse these two prepositions. *Since* signals time; it specifically signals the beginning of a continuous action or one that has happened at one time or another within a period. It means "from a past time to the present."

> Jeffrey has returned to his alma mater every year *since* he graduated.

Here Jeffrey engages in a continuous action of returning to his alma mater during a certain time period.

Because signals cause and effect or a reason for an action. It means "for the reason that."

> Leslie sold her shop *because* she was no longer making money.

Clearly, the action was the effect of losing money.

> Why did Jack climb the beanstalk? Because he wanted the giant's money.

Because he wanted the giant's money may be the correct answer, but it is not a sentence. Blame the plasticity of your brain for that mistake.

Adjective clauses

This clause modifies a noun or pronoun. The relative pronouns *who, which,* and *that* are the words usually used to introduce adjective clauses, but sometimes they are introduced by the relative adverbs *when, where,* and *why.*

> Some people *who invest in the stock market* are interested in the excitement of the trade more than the money.

The relative pronoun *who* introduces the restrictive adjective clause, which modifies the subject *people.* In this case the clause is restrictive because it is necessary to the meaning of the sentence. Without the clause the reader would not understand the context of *trade* and *money.*

> Today was a perfect day *when everything went right.*

When is a relative adverb that introduces an adjective clause, which modifies *day.*

Noun clauses

These clauses function as nouns, reminding us of a line from Irving Berlin's *Annie Get Your Gun,* "I can do anything you can do . . . ;" noun phrases can do anything nouns can do. They can be subjects, objects, objects of prepositions, predicate nominatives, adjective clauses, appositives, or adverb clauses. Most of the time noun clauses are introduced by *that, whatever, whoever, who, what, why, when, where,* and *whether.*

• Remember:

When people wonder how an adverb can be in an adjective clause, we say, always look to the function—the entire clause functions as an adjective.

> *Whatever you want for your birthday* is fine with me.

Here *whatever you want for your birthday* is a noun clause as subject.

> Her mother spent *whatever she had saved up for years.*

Whatever she had saved up for years is the noun clause as object.

> We are interested in *whatever our students are doing.*

In this sentence *whatever our students are doing* is a noun clause as object of the preposition.

> Whatever is worth doing well is *whatever is worth doing at all.*

Here we find *whatever is worth doing at all* as a predicate nominative.

> The car dealership *that sold the most cars* ended up bankrupt.

Here the noun clause *that sold the most cars* is used as an adjective.

> Nancy, *whoever replaces her*, will always be remembered.

Whoever replaces her is the noun clause as an appositive.

> *Since she began that computer course*, she has become a whiz at the keyboard.

In this sentence the noun clause *since she began that computer course* acts as adverb.

Absolute clauses and phrases

These are terms used interchangeably as they are a group of words that modify the entire independent clause. They always contain a noun or noun equivalent and a participial phrase. They can appear anywhere in the sentence.

> *Baring its teeth and snapping, the dog attacked the thief.*
>
> *The dog, baring its teeth and snapping, attacked the thief.*

• Remember:

Clauses can be combined in a variety of ways within a sentence.

Teaching Phrases and Clauses

1. The best way to teach phrases and clauses is by writing, getting students to write them, lots of them. After teaching and modeling each of the phrases and clauses, arm students with sentence strips and a challenge. They are to find in their reading, writing, or in mentor texts examples of each of the phrases and clauses they were taught. They may also write their own examples.

2. A variation of #1 is to invite students to copy the phrases and clauses in their original context on the sentence strips, underlining but not identifying the phrase or clause. Then they exchange strips. The person receiving the strip identifies the phrases and clauses. When finished, the identifier returns the strips to the originator to be checked. Share.

3. Phrase Ping-Pong gets all the students into the action.

    • Students are divided in triads: One person is the timer; the other two are players.

    • The teacher gives the directions. For example, "You are playing off the word *school*. All the phrases must be prepositional and relate to school, e.g., in the schoolyard, at my desk, on the board, behind the computer."

- One student "serves" and the "phrase ping pong ball" is hit back and forth until time is called or someone misses. (Thirty seconds works but the time is up to the teacher.)
4. Clause BINGO gets students into their writing and reading.
   - One way to play clause BINGO is to make up cards with a variety of prompts that demand clauses: Restrictive, unrestrictive, relative, and so forth. Mix them so each card is different. Mark the center square FREE. Students

fig. 7.1

find examples of each within a given time period. Then play BINGO. Decide on one horizontal row or one vertical row, postage stamp, four corners, and so forth. The teacher calls out prompts such as, "Under C, a restrictive clause; under E, a dependent clause . . ." until someone calls out BINGO! Then the clauses are checked for accuracy.

- The other way to play clause BINGO is to have the students create the cards, exchange them, and proceed as above.

5. For an in-depth, hands-on lesson on clauses, see Carroll's *Authentic Strategies for High-stakes Tests*, 40–49.

HERE WE GO A-SENTENCING:

SENTENCES AND HOW TO DIAGRAM THEM

> "It is not of so much con-
> sequence what you say, as
> how you say it. Memorable
> sentences are memorable on
> account of some single irra-
> diating word."
> —Alexander Smith

Sentence Sense

Once upon a time we undertook an analysis of text-book definitions for *sentences*. Surely, we thought, this aspect of grammar, taken for granted by so many, this most familiar of all grammatical terms, would have a definitive definition. What we discovered surprised us. In a nutshell, here is a sampling of what we found:

Some of these definitions are incorrect or partially correct. Consider the "complete thought." Many sentences are simply snippets "Tennis?" or interjections "Help!" In their context, the meaning is crystal clear.

- Some books give no definition, rather they launch into *syntax,* saying things like "The study of sentence structure is called *syntax.*"
- Several texts describe sentences but do not define them.
- Some wax poetic, "A sentence is a collection of words strung together like beads on a string."
- Many give the traditional definition we all remember, "A sentence expresses a complete thought."
- Others opt for structure, "A sentence contains a subject and a predicate."
- One cavalier definition states, "The term *sentence* refers to something punctuated as a sentence, with a beginning capital letter and an end mark of punctuation."
- Of course we found the wordy one, "A sentence is a grammatically self-contained group of words that expresses an assertion, a question, a command, a wish, or an exclamation that in writing usually begins with a capital letter and concludes with appropriate end punctuation, and that in speaking is phonetically distinguished by various patterns of stress, pitch, and pauses."
- We also found this "oops" one, "The basic English sentence is a sequence of phrases."

Many sentences express more than one thought. For instance: "For his birthday, Von wants a bike, a computer game, and a trip to Six Flags." There are at least three, maybe four thoughts in that sentence: birthday, bike, computer game, trip—maybe even Von himself and his wishes.

The "beads on a string," while a nice image, doesn't help anyone get a true handle on the concept. The "subject and predicate" definition is correct, but the abstractness of the language leaves many flummoxed.

The "capital letter/terminal punctuation" ignores the fact that many forms of writing do not use punctuation marks such as public notices, newspaper headlines (which are often in sentence form), or even some legal documents. People (and textbooks) don't always agree how to punctuate because many sentences may be punctuated differently. Take the great American author William Faulkner who sometimes ignores punctuation totally.

Pages and pages in the "Quentin" section go unpunctuated in his classic *The Sound and the Fury*.

Faulkner may have ignored punctuation from time to time for rhetorical effect, but that final "oops" definition just ignores altogether the possibility of clauses in a sentence.

Forced to draw a conclusion, we determined that English sentences are like boxes of breakfast cereals. They come in a variety of lengths, forms, and fit a variety of tastes. Even one word or a phrase may be considered irregular *minor sentences* such as "Exit" or "Fire! or "No parking." Interjections are often minor sentences. *Ow!* says it all. Our point is an absolute definition of the sentence eludes us. But we can and must talk about sentences. Two ways to do that is by function and type. There are four functions and four types, so remember the number four. We also talk about the structure of sentences.

The Four Functions of Sentences

entences have four functions or purposes. They make statements, ask questions, issue commands, and express emotions.

Declarative sentences

If a sentence makes a statement, we call it *declarative*. This makes sense because making a statement is declaring something. Declarative sentences end with a period.

> We are going to the park tomorrow to ride our bicycles.

Interrogative sentences

If a sentence asks a question, we call it *interrogative*. This also makes sense because to interrogate someone is to ask them questions. Interrogative sentences end with a question mark.

> Do you know what the weather report is for tomorrow?

Imperative sentences

If a sentence gives a command or order or makes a request, we call it *imperative*. This makes sense because the etymology of the word is the Latin *imperare*, which means to command. It is interesting to note that *emperor* comes from the same Latin word. Imperative sentences end with a period or an exclamation mark.

> Gerry, please go to the garage and get my bicycle.

> Gerry, please go to the garage and get my bicycle!

> (You) Please go to the garage and get my bicycle.

• Remember:

Imperative sentences often use the "you understood" subject.

Exclamatory sentences

If the sentence shows strong or sudden feeling or emotion, we call it *exclamatory*. This makes sense because when we exclaim we cry out suddenly or vehemently. Exclamatory sentences end with an exclamation mark.

> My bicycle is missing!

If an interjection comes first in an exclamatory sentence, it may be followed by an exclamation mark. Then the sentence ends with a period.

> Oh! my bicycle is missing.

If the interjection is followed by a comma, the sentence ends with an exclamation mark.

> Oh, my bicycle is missing!

Here we find Ruthie engaged in conversation with her grandmother. Typical of her generation, Rose asks Ruthie to

fig. 8.1 By permission of Rick Detorie and Creators Syndicate, Inc.

define the four types [functions] of sentences. Ruthie gives the terms she has learned. Rose is flabbergasted and responds accordingly. Then Ruthie proves she not only knows the functions of sentences but also can recognize them. Go, Ruthie!

The Four Types of Sentences

emember the "sanity clause"? Everything about the structure of sentences rests on the clause—how many and what type. When analyzing the structure of sentences, phrases don't count, just clauses matter.

Simple sentences

Are just that—simple. They have one independent clause and no subordinate clauses, but they may have phrases or even compound subjects and predicates, but they only have one independent clause.

Stan drove.

Stan drove his car.

Stan drove his car to the mall.

Stan drove his car to the mall with his sister.

Stan and Irene drove.

Stan and Irene drove to the mall.

Stan and Irene drove to the mall with their sister.

Stan drove and parked.

Stan drove and parked his car.

Stan drove and parked his car at the mall.

All these sentences are simple because each one contains only one independent clause.

• Remember:

Phrases don't count; there can be one or several.

Compound sentences

Compound sentences combine two simple sentences; therefore, we say they have two independent clauses with no subordinate clauses. These two clauses are joined with a comma and one of those *F A N B O Y S*, coordinating conjunctions, or by a semicolon.

The mall was crowded, but Stan found the "Eating Court."

The mall was crowded is one independent clause. *Stan found the "Eating Court"* is the second independent clause. They are joined with a comma and the coordinating conjunction *but*.

The mall was crowded; Stan found the "Eating Court."

Here the two independent clauses are joined with a semicolon. Don't be fooled by something like this:

> I ran up the stairs and entered my room.

While *I ran up the stairs* is an independent clause, *entered my room* is not. There is no subject. That construction holds a compound predicate; it is not a compound sentence.

Complex sentences

These do what they promise; they add complexity. Their structure allows for thought with more intricacy. A complex sentence has one independent clause, which is easy, but complicates the sentence by adding one or more subordinate clauses.

> After they went to the mall, Stan and Irene headed home.

> Stan and Irene headed home after they went to the mall.

After they went to the mall is the subordinate clause introduced by the subordinating conjunction *after,* and *Stan and Irene headed home* is the independent clause. Notice when the subordinate clause comes first in the sentence, it is followed by a comma. No comma is needed when it tags along at the end of the sentence.

Compound/complex sentences

These sentences are a combo platter. They contain at least two independent clauses (like a compound sentence) and at least one subordinate clause (like a complex sentence).

> As Stan and Irene left the mall, their car broke down, so they called their parents.

As Stan and Irene left the mall is the subordinate clause introduced by the subordinate conjunction *as.* Both *their car broke*

A compound sentence must have two independent clauses.

Remember:

If two independent clauses are joined with a comma, we call it a comma splice—a big no-no!

And if two independent clauses run into each other without punctuation, we call it a run-on or a fused sentence—a bigger no-no!

Remember:

AAA, BB, TUTU, IS, 6 Ws. These introduce subordinate clauses.

Independent
clauses can stand
alone, but those
dependent or
subordinate
clauses cannot.

down and *they called their parents* are independent clauses joined by a comma and the subordinating conjunction *so*.

The Structure of Sentences: Subjects, Predicates, Objects

Sentences, like everything from buildings to bicycles, have a structure. So another way to talk about sentences— usually in academic settings because people, unless they are English teachers, rarely gather to talk about sentences—is by their structure. Teachers and students use academic language to discuss subjects, predicates, and objects.

Subjects

Grammatically, all sentences have a subject, simple or complete, which announces the topic. Always nouns or pronouns, plus any words, phrases, or clauses that modify the subject, the subject controls the sentence and often the sentences that follow, but the speaker or writer's intention controls the subject. To find the simple subject, take away all modifiers, and there it will be. Consider how Bette Davis, the American actress on TV and in film, controlled her subject and notice how in turn her subject controlled the sentences that followed:

> "The weak are the most treacherous of us all. They come to the strong and drain them. They are bottomless. They are insatiable. They are always parched and always bitter. They are everyone's concern and like vampires they suck our life's blood" (Davis, 1962, ?).

Clearly *the weak* is the simple subject. Davis uses it as a collective noun, but she wants us to consider the individual members of that group, so that collective noun *the weak* determines the verb *are*. The pronominal chain of *they* as continuous subjects connects *the weak* to all that follows in a coherent way.

Predicates

Predicates tell more about the subject, comment on the subject, or provide the action of the subject. Logically, predicates affirm or deny something about the subject; grammatically, predicates always contain a verb.

Let's look at the predicates in Davis's excerpt. The simple predicates *are*—linking verbs—show existence. *Come* and *drain* are powerful compound verbs in Davis's context, and then we read that corker *suck*. But the predicate adjectives— those words that describe her subject *the weak*—those words coming after the linking verbs—they provide her commentary: *most treacherous, bottomless, insatiable, always parched and always bitter, everyone's concern*. These predicate adjectives, sometimes called adjective complements, as part of the predicate are both telling and terrible in conveying and completing her commentary.

fig. 8.2 "Frank and Ernest" reprinted by permission. United Artists.
© Bob Thaves. www.comics.com

"Frank and Ernest" by Bob Thaves chronicles everyday people observing everyday events. In this cartoon the observation is about English teachers who never miss the opportunity to teach.

Objects

Some sentences have objects.

Direct objects—the *what* or *who*—are nouns or pronouns that receive the *direct* action of the verb.

> Indirect objects—the *to whom* or *for whom*—are nouns or pronouns that tell to or for whom the action is done; therefore, they are *indirect*.
>
> Subjective or objective complements complete the meaning of the subject or complete the meaning of the direct object.

In the Davis excerpt, we find the prepositional object, most often called the object of the preposition, *to the strong*. We also find the direct object *our life's blood* in the independent clause *like vampires they suck our life's blood*. After a comparison to vampires, the direct object tells us the *what* of the *weak*—they suck what? *Our life's blood*.

Six basic sentence structures

S-V	SUBJECT-VERB
S-V-DO	SUBJECT-VERB-DIRECT OBJECT
S-V-IO-DO	SUBJECT-VERB-INDIRECT OBJECT-DIRECT OBJECT
S-V-PN	SUBJECT-VERB-PREDICATE NOMINATIVE
S-V-PA	SUBJECT-VERB-PREDICATE ADJECTIVE
S-V-DO-C	SUBJECT-VERB-DIRECT OBJECT-COMPLEMENTS

Subject/Verb Agreement

We like to think of subject/verb agreement as a seesaw with the subject and verb teeter tottering on each end of the plank. On one end sits the subject; on the other end sits the verb. The subject of the sentence decides which side goes up in the air. If the controlling noun in the subject is singular with no *s*, the verb generally adds an *s* or *es*, gets "heavier," and down it goes!

fig. 8.3

> Mary loves the playground.

If the subject is heavier, carrying the *s* or *es* as a plural, it goes down, and the lighter verb without the *s* or *es* flies up.

> The neighborhood kids love the playground.

fig. 8.4

Problems happen when intervening words, phrases, or clauses are inserted that cause confusion. Typically items on tests do that. For example:

> Mary, who lives with her three sisters, loves the playground.

Reading *sisters* so close to the verb *love* confuses the subject for many, so the test taker might choose *love* to agree with sisters not *loves* to agree with Mary, the true subject.

Sentence Fragments

The biggest problem surrounding sentences happens when a sentence isn't a sentence at all. We call these bits and pieces *fragments*. If a sentence lacks a subject (unless it is "you understood"), it is a fragment. If it lacks a verb (here's where those verbals cause trouble), it is a fragment. If it is a subordinate/dependent clause (with a subject and a verb), it is a fragment.

Over the years we have categorized reasons for fragments:

- lack of understanding of the concept of a sentence;
- inability to punctuate;
- rhetorical emphasis;
- the "because clause" syndrome;
- carelessness.

To find the subject always look for the "doer" of the action.

Strip everything else away and the agreement should become clear by applying the see-saw idea.

Lack of understanding simply means the person has no sentence sense. This phenomenon is actually quite rare.

Inability to punctuate has nothing to do with sentence sense and everything to do with punctuation.

Rhetorical emphasis allows people to write fragments if they work in the context.

The "because clause" syndrome happens when the question asked demands a "because" answer. The "because clause" looks like a sentence; it has a subject and verb, but the *because* makes it a subordinate clause. Sometimes this gets embedded in our brains and "seems" correct.

> Why would you drive to the mall if you were low on gas? Because my friends were there.

Because my friends were there is so seductive; it seems like a legitimate sentence, but without the question, it has no context and remains dependent.

Carelessness occurs when the writer relies on spoken language to influence written language and does not go back to reread what has come out of the head; therefore, the fragment, while in spoken language would connect, in written language just rests in the paragraph like some unclaimed piece of luggage.

fig. 8.5 By permission of Rick Detorie and Creators Syndicate, Inc.

Joe, age eight, attempts to give an example of a sentence for his dad. He puzzles for a frame and then gives his response. Ah! those multi-meaning words will do it every time.

Diagramming Sentences

E.B. White, one of our heroes, while reaching for a metaphor for grammar and more likely diagramming said, "No ball game is anything but chaotic if it lacks a mound, a box, bases, and foul lines" (Florey, 30). That metaphor suggests the need for organization—tight, predictable organization. Apparently a teacher named Stephen Clark, one hundred years before White, thought so, too. He likened grammar to geometry and architecture as he created a new way to teach grammar—diagramming. His "bubbles" so revolutionized the teaching of grammar, which had been taught solely through the deadly and deadening parsing of each word in a sentence, that Clark's colleagues at the Cortland Academy in Homer, New York, reportedly clamored for his technique. He wrote a book and began a craze.

Clark's method looks different than today's concept of diagramming. Picture a series of dirigibles of various sizes floating in space with words within them. If you read the word-carrying blimps in the right order, you discover a sentence. Surely the novelty effect kicked in as students played with Clark's "bubbles" and surely teachers, unshackled from the bonds of parsing (which depended so much on context and often defied right or wrong), embraced the method as an easier way to analyze sentences.

This happened in the 1840s!

Clark was on to something thought Alonzo Reed and Brainerd Kellogg, lecturers and professors, respectively, at Brooklyn Polytechnic Institute. These two men straightened out those nice round "bubbles," writing books on diagramming, and becoming wealthy in the process.

They titled their book *Higher Lessons in English.* Revised in 1887, its title page states: *A Work on English Grammar and Composition, in which the Science of the Language is made tributary to the Art of Expression. A course of practical lessons carefully guided, and adapted to everyday use in the school-room.* Now that title alone would most assuredly impress parents and scare the beeswax out of students.

Interestingly, it is still available. Go to Amazon!

What makes diagramming so appealing? What killed diagramming? We decided to tackle these two questions.

The appeal of diagramming

- First and perhaps foremost, diagramming is fun!
- Making something as abstract as grammar concrete holds appeal. Carroll did a lot of diagramming in "grammar school." She loved "rulering" of all those lines and thinking if she somehow got the right words on the right lines, she knew her grammar. Maybe she did. She is co-authoring this book after all.
- The brain research on visualizing and manipulating supports diagramming. To be able to see where parts of a sentence go and manipulate them in relation to other parts moves concepts from the short-term (fill in a worksheet) memory to the working memory to the long-term memory.
- The brain also revels in challenge, and diagramming presents a challenge. Each sentence is different, so each diagram is different.
- Diagramming is an act of linguistic discipline. It demystifies the English language.
- Diagramming is easy to assess; it's the old right or wrong paradigm.
- Diagramming is like a game—right or wrong, win or lose, get the subject and find the verb. This appeals to the linear thinker, the left-brain learner.
- Finally, diagramming impresses parents and most everyone else.

The downside of diagramming

- There is little evidence that proves diagramming helps writing, and it may really hurt the act of writing.
- Diagramming may not really help our true, deeper grasp of grammar.
- Learning to diagram actually increases what kids have to learn—not only do they have to learn the definition and function of a direct object, for example, but also they have to learn where it goes on the line and what kind of line precedes, follows, or hangs off it.
- Sentences for diagramming sometimes seem stilted compared to the wonderful flexibility of our language.
- Just as diagramming appeals to the left-brain learner, it is deadly for the right-brainer.

- Students don't have to diagram sentences to learn grammar. They have to write.
- There are precious few jobs where people have to label the parts of a sentence, but in today's global society most jobs require effective communicators.
- Diagramming can be boring, stressful, and confusing.
- Finally, teachers must spend valuable instructional time teaching the rudiments of diagramming, all the lines and angles, which could be better spent teaching writing or certain aspects of grammar.

fig. 8.6 "Frank and Ernest" reprinted by permission. United Artists.
© Bob Thaves. www.comics.com

Thaves places diagramming in the real world of economics. A budding capitalist asks her teacher a practical question, which got us to thinking. What *does* a diagrammer pull down a year?

To diagram or not to diagram, that is the question

Actually lots of adults maintain that they loved diagramming sentences in school (of course, many also screw up their faces in remembered angst). So what killed diagramming? Teachers murdered a good idea by cooking up those impossibly long sentences, by assigning fifty diagrams for homework, or by giving students nonsensical exercises such as *Declaration of Independence* or the first chapter of *Genesis* to diagram. What initially worked, perhaps because of the novelty effect, fanned our zeal; we became diagramming zealots who systematically slaughtered a successful strategy with "too muchness"; we bludgeoned it to death with our red pens.

So why do we have diagramming in this book? We believe no single strategy works for every person every time, but we do believe that some strategies work for some people some of the time. Diagramming provides a balance between total expressive freedom and the skills people need to effectively do just that. (See Appendix A)

Snip, snap, snout,

This work on sentences is told out

Teaching Sentences: Two Ideas

1. Sentence pop-up books. We like to teach students the four functions of sentences with pop-up books. Then we invite students to apply their knowledge of sentences by constructing three-dimensional (3-D) books for the four sentence structures. As they work through how to construct their three-dimensional books, their brains work through how the sentence itself is structured. Make no mistake: this is the same process Clark, Reed, and Kellogg went through as they created their "bubbles" and decided what would go where as they developed the diagram.

Sentence pop-up books

- Four sheets of heavyweight 8.5″ x 11″ paper in four different colors.
- Fold the sheets in half, short end to short end.
- Taking each sheet separately, place the ruler slightly below the fold, measure in 1.5″, and mark.
- From that first mark continue to mark parallel to the fold 2″, 2″, 2″ with 1″ remaining.
- Cut from the fold on the 1.5″ mark and on the second, third, and fourth marks.
- Bend those two 2″ boxes back and forth.
- Push each 2″ in and press down. When both 2″ sections are pressed in, the sheet forms the letter *E*.
- Paste the back of one sheet to the front of another to make the book.

Text for the sentence pop-up books

- This book opens horizontally.
- Younger students label the cover "Kinds of Sentences" or "Types of Sentences"; older students label it "Functions of Sentences." They place their name on the cover.

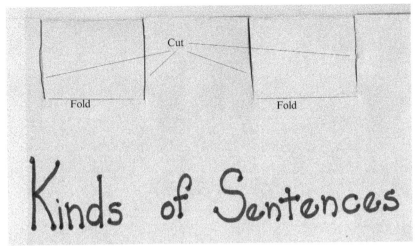

fig. 8.7

- Above the two boxes on the first page, students write the definition:
    A declarative sentence declares or tells something. It makes a statement.
- Above the first box they write:
    It begins
- On the flat top of the first box they write:
    with a capital letter
- On the side of the box that pops out, they make a large capital C.
- On the crease between the boxes they write the word *and.*
- Above the second box they write the word *ends.*
- On the flat top of the second box they write:
    with a period.
- On the side of the box that pops out, they make a large dot.
- In the remaining space below the two boxes, they write:
    Find it in your writing:
- They leave a space and then write:
    Find it in your reading:
- They proceed to the other three functions of sentences, following the same format.
- When the book is complete, they re-enter it, finding and filling in the spaces from their writing and reading. When they do this they are applying their knowledge to authentic language experiences—not some phony sentences on a worksheet.

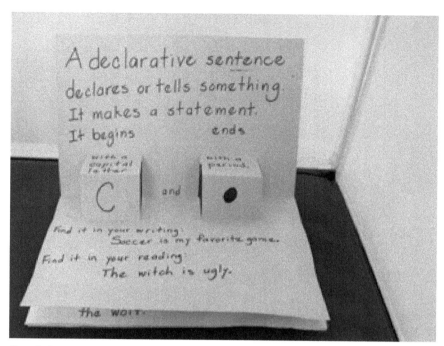

fig. 8.8

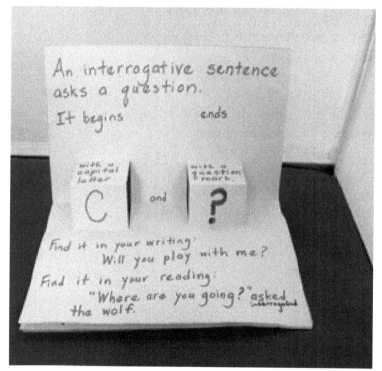

fig. 8.9

An imperative sentence gives directions or makes a command. It begins ... ends ...

with a capital letter

C

and

with a period or an exclamation mark.

. !

Find it in your writing: Go to the end of the line!

Find it in your reading: "Put your baseball glove on," commanded the coach.

fig. 8.10

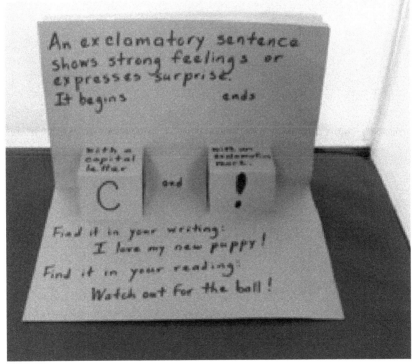

An exclamatory sentence shows strong feelings or expresses surprise. It begins ... ends ...

with a capital letter

C

and

with an exclamation mark.

!

Find it in your writing: I love my new puppy!

Find it in your reading: Watch out for the ball!

fig. 8.11

2. 3-D Diagramming

Students may also create three-dimensional pages modeled after the one-dimensional diagram. They use colored paper, brads, clips, tape, and glue. They layer the paper or juxtapose it to show how parts of the sentence relate to other parts. We have had students make flips and flaps and wheels all the while discussing the structure of sentences. When we invite students to do this, they are free to demonstrate not only their knowledge of grammar but also their ingenuity and resourcefulness.

TOOLS OF THE TRADE:

PARAGRAPHS, PUNCTUATION, AND CAPITAL LETTERS

> "Paragraphs are not composed; they are discovered. To compose is to create; to indent is to interpret."
> —Paul Rodgers

Composition scholars the ilk of Pat Belanoff, Betsy Rorschach, Paul Rodgers, and Donald Murray consider indenting a form of punctuation. "We like to think of paragraphs as higher-order punctuation marks that extend the connections shown by commas, semi-colons, and periods" (Belanoff, Rorschach, and Oberlink, 22). That's why we grouped paragraphs with punctuation. Both are tools used by writers to help ease communication. A well-placed comma clarifies; an indention specifies.

Planning Paragraphs

Think of a composition as the act of putting parts together, and think of paragraphs as those parts. Research tells us that the word *composition* comes from the Latin *compositio* meaning *to put together*. The word *paragraph* comes from the Latin *pararaphus,* a sign used to mark a new section of writing—technically *para*—beside and *graphein*—to write. Not so incidentally this mark, the pilcrow (¶), is still used to show typesetters where to indent the type. Over time writers adapted the Greek's *paragraphos,* the device of drawing a line to show a break in sense or a change of speakers, to our notion of indention—no line but a space as the signal.

Indenting is one thing, but putting it together takes some skill. Check out Stephen Sondheim's lyrics for "Putting It Together" in *Sunday in the Park with George.* Although Sondheim's song pertains to color and design in art, the overarching concept holds in writing. Success depends on how the writer puts the paragraphs together.

Paragraphs thrown together haphazardly like so many coins in a bowl leave the reader confused, but paragraphs organized according to the rules of logic leave the reader informed.

Because paragraphs encapsulate the writer's ideas, how the writer plans paragraphs or goes back after the piece is written to organize or reorganize them radiates around the writer's intention. Paragraphs may be long to capture a complex idea, they may be short and emphatic for rhetorical effect, or they may be any length in between for many different reasons.

Randomly open a book of any genre. We bet the paragraphs on that page will vary in length. Like the writer's thoughts, some paragraphs stretch out an idea, others compress it.

The Grammar of Paragraphs

Usually when we think of paragraphs the word *grammar* doesn't pop into our heads. Yet one definition of *grammar* is "a set of elements or basic fundamental principles."

In the case of paragraphs, these fundamentals are what make a paragraph a paragraph. Six elements comprise the grammar of paragraphs.

1. Unity
2. Coherence
3. Visual effectiveness
4. Structural effectiveness
5. Depth of thought
6. Placement

Whatever its length, every paragraph signals the reader, a signal that promises these six fundamentals.

Unity

A reader approaches a paragraph expecting it to be about one thing—not a jumble of thoughts, stream of consciousness, or random snippets. When a paragraph stays on one topic, has a governing purpose, we say it is unified. We achieve unity in a paragraph through a repetition of major words and phrases, synonyms or even antonyms, and pronominal chains and their antecedents. Without unity the reader may be confused, frustrated, or even angry at having to work so hard to figure out the writer's intent.

Coherence: Internal/external

Another expectation a reader brings to the paragraph is that its sentences will hang together, each new sentence connecting in some way to the sentence that came before it. When sentences connect one to the next, we call this *internal coherence*.

Then when the reader comes to the next paragraph, the expectation is that the paragraph just read will connect in some way to the one about to be read. When paragraphs connect one to the next, we call this *external coherence*. We achieve coherence through the linking of ideas in logical ways and through transitions, which act as reminders, short strings tied onto the fingers of a paragraph to connect ideas.

Visual and structural effectiveness
Visual effectiveness

In today's fast-paced, text-message, instant-replay world, we are attracted to something that has more white space, something that tells us we can quickly and easily "get it." We call this *visual effectiveness*. Less text, or the illusion of less text, seems more inviting than pages and pages of dense text. Recently we came across a 1940s ad for Palmolive soap. With a picture of the signature green-colored soap at the top of the page as the only eye relief, the text explaining the advantages of using Palmolive went on relentlessly for the entire page. One of us quipped, "Today no one would take the time to read that!" Advertisers know that, so they work hard to make their messages appealing. That principle also applies to paragraphs.

Visually, paragraphs should attract, not dissuade the reader. Besides, tight unified coherent writing better holds the reader's attention.

Structural effectiveness

Structural effectiveness speaks to purpose. Always and in all ways, the structure of a paragraph should match its development. Following are nutshell structures.

- *Deductive* paragraphs start with a broad, general statement followed by details, examples, illustrations, and other kinds of support. We call these *whole-to-part* paragraphs.
- *Inductive* paragraphs flip flop the deductive. They begin with the details or examples and move toward the closing generalization. We call these *parts-to-whole* paragraphs.
- *Descriptive* paragraphs are blocks of images. We call these *picture-in-words* paragraphs.
- *Narrative* paragraphs tell a wee story. We call these *anecdotal* paragraphs.
- *Process* paragraphs assemble stages or steps. We call these *step-by-step* paragraphs.

- *Comparison/Contrast* paragraphs define or describe by telling what something is or is not. We call these *A/B* paragraphs.
- *Analogy* paragraphs make connections. We call these *extended simile* paragraphs.
- *Classification* paragraphs divide something into its parts. We call these *analytic* paragraphs.
- *Cause/Effect* paragraphs explore. We call these *what happened?* paragraphs.
- *Persuasive* paragraphs implore. We call these *consider this* paragraphs.

Depth of thought

Paragraphs, chunks of thought orchestrated to make sense for the reader, may be various lengths with various structures based upon various purposes. The point, after all, is to communicate. The notion of formulaic paragraphs and rigid forms actually shackles the writer who tries to fit meaning into form rather than finding a form to fit meaning. Following formula does not really teach the writer the grammar of a paragraph but rather uses a crutch that generally results in poor writing. The critics who justify poor pedagogy with the rationale that bilingual and minority writers have to have "Structure," with a capital *S* do not understand true structure, so they ensure these writers never participate freely in communicating the meaning of their own discourse.

Determining how a paragraph might persuade, inform, compare, define happens after the prewriting. Through prewriting the author finds the footing upon which to build, and then the apt grammar of the paragraph may be chosen. Matching meaning and form illuminates the depth of thought *and* voice of the writer.

Placement

A paragraph works (or not) in relation to the paragraphs that come before and after it. A paragraph is not a solitary unit, but a paragraph among paragraphs. Seeing it in relation to its placement allows it to fully function with the first five elements.

Sara Rueter, a master teacher, worked with Scott, a twelfth-grade student on his college admission essay. A powerful and

• Remember:

These structures are not absolute isolated units; good writers blend and blur, sometimes including within the bigger structure of a process paper, paragraphs that contain comparison/contrast or description or both. It is a fallacy to think of these structures as static; they are dynamic and give the writer choice.

authentic piece of writing built upon the sacrifices of his immigrant family, Scott wrote with voice and style. Still, at first he placed what became his last paragraph second. It diluted its poignancy. Sara conferred with Scott and suggested that he try reformulating the placement of his paragraphs. He did. We are not certain moving that paragraph sealed the vote, but we are certain Scott was unanimously accepted into Harvard.

Transitions

Transitions come in three sizes. In a sense they are like the *Three Billy Goats Gruff*: small, big, huge. One word, a phrase, clause, several sentences, or even an entire paragraph may function as a transition.

Transitions are the "Janus" of composition. Artists and sculptures usually depict the Roman god Janus as facing backward and forward. That is exactly what transitions do. They help the reader focus in two directions, backward and forward. Paragraphs build upon what came before but move the reader forward. This backward/forward momentum depends upon several things:

- transitional terms that indicate location, time, cause/effect, addition, example, alternatives, time, and conclusion
- explicit and implicit logical connections
- parallel or similar sentence structures
- pronouns—less emphatic than nouns so they bear up under repetition, but they ask the audience to remember their antecedents. That is why getting pronouns to correctly agree with their antecedents is so important.

Analyzing the Grammar of the Paragraph in *The Gettysburg Address*

L et's analyze one of the most famous speeches in American history *The Gettysburg Address* for its grammar of paragraphs. In three paragraphs written by Lincoln (not speechwriters) and taking about two minutes to deliver, Lincoln produced the perfect mentor text for analyzing the grammar of paragraphs.

To better understand its brilliance, let's put it in a context. The date was November 19, 1863; the site Gettysburg, Pennsylvania. Lincoln commemorated the cemetery there where more than 51,000 Union *and* Confederate soldiers had died in battle. This historic battle ended Lee's invasion of the North, but Lincoln chose to focus not on the Union victory but on the principles of liberty and equality. The speech contains ten sentences, 262 words.

> Four score and seven years ago our fathers brought forth on this continent, a new nation, conceived in Liberty, and dedicated to the proposition that all men are created equal.
>
> Now we are engaged in a great civil war, testing whether that nation, or any nation so conceived and so dedicated, can long endure. We are met on a great battlefield of that war. We have come to dedicate a portion of that field, as a final resting place for those who here gave their lives that that nation might live. It is altogether fitting and proper that we should do this.
>
> But, in a larger sense, we cannot dedicate—we cannot consecrate—we cannot hallow—this ground. The brave men, living and dead, who struggled here, have consecrated it, far above our poor power to add or detract. The world will little note, nor long remember what we say here, but it can never forget what they did here. It is for us the living, rather, to be dedicated here to the unfinished work, which they who fought here have thus far so nobly advanced. It is rather for us to be here dedicated to the great task remaining before us—that from these honored dead we take increased devotion to that cause for which they gave the last full measure of devotion—that we here highly resolve that these dead shall not have died in vain—that this nation, under God, shall have a new birth of freedom—and that government of the people, by the people, for the people, shall not perish from the earth.

The first paragraph

In the first paragraph, which is one sentence (dispelling for all time the notion that a paragraph cannot be one sentence), Lincoln hooks his audience with the lead phrase "Four score and seven years" a clear allusion to Psalm 90:10 "three score year and ten" thought of as the life span of a person, an allusion familiar to his audience. Through that allusion Lincoln tells his audience that while the country has already outlived the life of one person, it is still young.

The allusion also refers to signing of the *Declaration of Independence,* which happened exactly eighty-seven years prior to this speech and links that lead phrase to the rest of the sentence with *brought forth, conceived,* and *created,* words synonymous with birth. Stunningly coherent, Lincoln then glues the notion of the birthing of a nation to the founding fathers and mother liberty. He quotes "all men are created equal" from the *Declaration of Independence* to point out that slavery goes against the founding principles of this country without actually saying the word *slavery.*

The speech's overall organization is chronological, its logic inductive. The first paragraph refers to the past, to the birth of the nation.

The second paragraph

The second paragraph, beginning with the word *now,* sets the time in the present where Lincoln continues the connection from the past to the imagery of a young growing nation with *conceived* and *that nation might live.* He emphasizes equality by repeating the word *we* four times. In rhetoric, this is called the "persuasive We." The first person plural helps the audience identify with the speaker. *We* becomes foundational here because Lincoln wants to establish common ground,

The third paragraph

Transitioning to the third paragraph and to the future, Lincoln uses the coordinating conjunction *but* and continues to repeat the word *we.* Interestingly, he uses a thesis/antithesis construct in the sentence

> *The world will little note nor long remember what we say here, but it can never forget what they did here.*

Aside from the irony that Lincoln's words live as one of the most eloquent, most quoted, most studied political speeches of all time, the *but* sets the two clauses in opposition to one another, suggesting the world is conflicted between words and deeds, yet Lincoln tells us that we remember deeds over words.

Finally, in that third paragraph, Lincoln surprisingly uses the passive voice twice! The phrase *to be dedicated* gains emphasis by its incremental repetition. First it refers to *the unfinished work;* then to *the great task.* Using the passive voice, though, places the burden on the *us.* His coherence is impeccable, repeating the word *devotion* and building upon those who gave their *last full measure of devotion* to *us the living* to bring about this *new birth of freedom.*

Now let's look at the speech as one paragraph.

> Four score and seven years ago our fathers brought forth on this continent, a new nation, conceived in Liberty, and dedicated to the proposition that all men are created equal. Now we are engaged in a great civil war, testing whether that nation, or any nation so conceived and so dedicated, can long endure. We are met on a great battlefield of that war. We have come to dedicate a portion of that field, as a final resting place for those who here gave their lives that that nation might live. It is altogether fitting and proper that we should do this. But, in a larger sense, we cannot dedicate—we cannot consecrate—we cannot hallow—this ground. The brave men, living and dead, who struggled here, have consecrated it, far above our poor power to add or detract. The world will little note, nor long remember what we say here, but it can never forget what they did here. It is for us the living, rather, to be dedicated here to the unfinished work, which they who fought here have thus far so nobly advanced. It is rather for us to be here dedicated to the great task remaining before us—that from these honored dead we take increased devotion to that cause for which they gave the last full measure of devotion—that we here highly resolve that these dead shall not have died in vain—that this nation, under God, shall have a new birth of freedom—and that government of the people, by the people, for the people, shall not perish from the earth.

Daunting, isn't it? Without the indentions, those visual clues, almost everything gets lost in the sense that nothing is outstandingly important.

If we divide the speech into two paragraphs, we see something else emerge.

Four score and seven years ago our fathers brought forth on this continent, a new nation, conceived in Liberty, and dedicated to the proposition that all men are created equal. Now we are engaged in a great civil war, testing whether that nation, or any nation so conceived and so dedicated, can long endure. We are met on a great battlefield of that war. We have come to dedicate a portion of that field, as a final resting place for those who here gave their lives that that nation might live. It is altogether fitting and proper that we should do this.

But, in a larger sense, we cannot dedicate—we cannot consecrate—we cannot hallow—this ground. The brave men, living and dead, who struggled here, have consecrated it, far above our poor power to add or detract. The world will little note, nor long remember what we say here, but it can never forget what they did here. It is for us the living, rather, to be dedicated here to the unfinished work, which they who fought here have thus far so nobly advanced. It is rather for us to be here dedicated to the great task remaining before us—that from these honored dead we take increased devotion to that cause for which they gave the last full measure of devotion—that we here highly resolve that these dead shall not have died in vain—that this nation, under God, shall have a new birth of freedom—and that government of the people, by the people, for the people, shall not perish from the earth.

The entire sense of the present is swallowed up. We are not sure where the past ends and the present begins. We have no transitional paragraph between the past and the future, so time runs together. Without indentation, the last sentence of the first paragraph reads more like a summary than part of the commemoration.

Teaching Paragraphs

Students using computer technology and *The Gettysburg Address* as a mentor text, take a piece of discourse written in multiple paragraphs according to the author's purpose and rearrange them to see how that simple act can influence the writer's intention and the reader's meaning. This is fun and productive to do in groups.

They soon discover that indention changes the rhetoric of the paragraph by causing some connections to seem more important or less important, by changing the focus, by muddling the organization, by blurring the time, or by losing key transitions. Indention may even alter the interpretation of first and last sentences.

After they have fiddled with several paragraphs, ask them to respond to Paul Rodgers, "Paragraphs are not composed; they are discovered. To compose is to create; to indent is to interpret."

Punctuation

> "I've always loved the flirtatious tango of consonants and vowels, the sturdy dependability of nouns and capricious whimsy of verbs, the strutting pageantry of the adjective and the flitting evanescence of the adverb, all kept safe and orderly by those reliable little policemen, punctuation marks. Wow!"
>
> —Dennis Miller

Miller nails it. Marching along with words come the punctuation police, keeping everything in order. They strengthen sentences, clarify meaning, and sometimes even help straighten out the lines of logic.

Like letters, words, and grammar, punctuation has a history. During the writing of many classical texts, we had no punctuation. Some students might wish they lived when texts were unpunctuated! But imagine reading an early classical text with no punctuation and no spaces between words, just letters from margin to margin, top to bottom.

Actually, the first marks were for public speakers. Later, markings as in Biblical texts helped reflect nuances. Then we moved into a period of extensive use of marking texts, but the punctuation was non-standardized. Finally, with the advent of the printing press, punctuation slowly became standardized although punctuation never achieved a level of total rule-governed consistency. This is due in part because so much of punctuation depends upon the intent of the author. In the second edition of *Acts of Teaching* we prove this with the simple sentence: *Tom Smith called Sarah Lou is here,* which can be correctly punctuated over seventy different ways.

By 1825, students were studying punctuation. Madame Leinstein wrote *The Good Child's Book of Stops: or, Punctuation in Verse* to help children learn the concepts of punctuation via "Mr. Stops" within whom were all the punctuation marks used at that time. In her book, Mr. Stops accompanies a series of poems, each giving advice about one punctuation mark. For example:

fig. 9.1

COMMA ,
At the *Comma* each reader should stay, and count *one*;
As,—Charles had an orange, a tart, and a bun.

Aside from the interruption of counting—one for commas, two for semicolons, three for colons, four for periods, exclamation points, and question marks, which undoubtedly interfered with comprehension not to mention fluency—these little verses read as forced doggerel and bad pedagogy. Still, we must consider the time period and give Madame Leinstein credit for trying to make punctuation interesting and visual for children. (We all remember how a mere twenty or so years later Charles Dickens satirized prescriptive grammarians and the suffering students they tormented.)

Looking at Mr. Stops we imagine children challenged to find commas, periods, semicolons, colons, periods, exclamation points, interrogation marks (question marks), apostrophes, quotation marks, dashes, hyphens, and parentheses. Perhaps the gifted students of the time even found parallels, grave and acute accents, and brackets.

Consider the fun students had locating in Mr. Stops the now passé section sign, the pointing hand (index or fist), the obelisk, which they probably called by its synonym *dagger*, as well as braces, the pilcrow, the three asterisks for ellipsis, which we now more often mark with three dots. We can almost hear the laughter when someone spotted the caret, cleverly sitting atop the head of Mr. Stops.

Upon our own discovery of Mr. Stops we asked ourselves, "When did this early 19th-century, colorful, visual approach to punctuation change to the drab, mindless, boring, repetitive worksheets we see in 21st-century classrooms?" Some authors interested in wooing students to love grammar—O'Connor, Truss, Pulver, Heller—and some academicians—Weaver, Noden, Smith and Wilhelm, Anderson, among others—have valiantly tried to make the subject interesting or at least palatable, but the dull, lifeless textbooks and un-green monotonous worksheets prevail.

The Four Functions of Punctuation

 ometimes underestimated, punctuation is crucial in writing and reading. To that end we have identified four functions of punctuation:

1. To enable long stretches of written text to be read according to the writer's intention. Punctuation tells us when to stop, when to pause, and when a new point is made. Especially important here are periods, commas, and indentions.
2. To give clues about what to emphasize, when to change intonations, who is speaking, especially if reading aloud. Here quotation marks, exclamation points, question marks, and parentheses gain importance.
3. To highlight units of language such as parallel structures, lines of poetry, or even grammatical structures. Colons, semicolons, and virgules help us here.
4. To add dimension to the written word through graphic symbols not read aloud. Examples include italics to show a word has a special sense or capital letters to underscore an important point.

Common Punctuation Marks

Periods (.)

Periods, also called full stops, full points, points, or the Latin *punctus,* identify the end of declarative and imperative sentences, abbreviated words, dates (9.24.09), money units, section numbers in books, and decimals. The Greeks used the word *periodos* to mean the way around a circuit, which accurately creates the image of the tiny circular dot.

• Remember:

Usually we do not put a period to abbreviate names of organizations, e.g., NATO, NAACP, IBM.

Question marks (?)

In John Hart's *The Opening of the Unreasonable Writing of our Inglish Toung* (1551), the question mark was called the "asker," which makes us wonder why a term so perfect ever changed. In terms of history, we go back to the *punctus interrogativus* of the 8th century. It was a wavy slanted line upward and right above the period. Linguists think it was designed to show the upward inflection of the speaking voice. Today we use the question mark to indicate a question, mark an uncertainty, or to signal irony or the astounded silence of Christopher Robin in *Winnie-the-Pooh.*

(A.A. Milne 1926, 144)

Not only does Milne use punctuation as punctuation, but also he uses it as dialogue.

Exclamation points (!)

Here we drop back in time again—this time to the 14th century and the *punctus exclamativus* or *punctus admirativus* where we find two points under a short line slanting to the right. Printers set the mark upright. Hart called this mark the "wonderer," but little children call it the excitement mark and often make a string of them when they write to intensify their feelings. The great A.A. Milne did it too, but generally one exclamation point does the job of showing force, surprise, sudden emotion.

We might go in your umbrella," said Pooh.
" !!!!!! "
For suddenly Christopher Robin saw that they might.
(A.A. Milne 1926, 144).

fig. 9.2 By permission of Rick Detorie and Creators Syndicate, Inc.

Rose has read Ruthie's story, one we know from working with young children is riddled with exclamation points. But

Nick used that moment to make an astute yet sad commentary on contemporary life.

Colons (:)

This 15th-century symbol marks major pauses. The word *colon* comes from the Greek, *kolon,* meaning "limb," "member," or "metrical unit." We use colons to precede an amplification of something, introduce examples, to formally introduce a quotation, separate numbers as in time (10:30), to separate titles from subtitles, to cite law or the Bible, between the publisher and the place of publication in a bibliography, or after formal salutations. In 1551 John Hart called the colon "joint."

The major use of the colon is before a list following an independent clause. Think of the independent clause as a path leading up to more information. Think of the colon as a gate that opens to that information; therefore, be sure an independent clause comes before a colon.

> The following people will remain on the stage: Marty, Joan, and Harold.

While we have a sense a list of people will come after that colon, *The following people will remain on the stage* is an independent clause.

> On the stage are Marty, Joan, and Harold.

No independent clause before the list of names, no colon.

Most people make the mistake of inserting a colon when there is no independent clause. Think of it this way: when there is no path, there is no need for a "gate," so do not use a colon.

> The repairs consisted of mending the broken windshield, fixing the flat, adjusting the steering wheel, and painting the fender.

The list is simply the object of the preposition *of*. *The repairs consisted of* is not an independent clause so no colon, no "gate" is needed.

A colon is often used in scripts following the name of the speaker.

> Sherlock: I have come to collect my fee.
> Antonia: You shall have it forthwith.

If the introductory phrase preceding the colon is very brief and the clause following the colon represents the real business of the sentence, begin the clause after the colon with a capital letter. Remember: Many of the prominent families of this New England state were slaveholders prior to 1850.

Semicolons (;)

Semicolons, dating back to the 15th century, mark a pause longer than a comma but shorter than a colon. Today semicolons signal the coordinate parts of a complex sentence, separate parts in a list, or replace the coordinate conjunction in a compound sentence. Throughout its history, the semicolon has carried different names to indicate that it is not quite a colon due to that dot directly above the comma: *comma-colon, semi-colon, or sub-colon*.

Most people use semicolons to join independent clauses as a replacement for a coordinating conjunction.

> Elyse is the oldest and smartest child in the family;
> Jeffrey is the youngest and the most successful.

Elyse is the oldest and smartest child in the family is one independent clause. *Jeffrey is the youngest and the most successful* is the second independent clause. The semicolon replaces the coordinating conjunction *and*. If the writer wanted to set up a thesis/antithesis, it would be best to use the *but* instead of the semicolon because the relationship would not be as clear without the conjunction.

Another common use of semicolons is before a conjunctive adverb that links independent clauses.

• Remember:

When an independent clause follows a colon, it may begin with an upper or lower case letter unless it is a quotation or more than one sentence.

> The Rockets play basketball like true pros; however, the Spurs usually win the NBA playoffs.

The Rockets play basketball like true pros is one independent clause. *The Spurs usually win the NBA playoffs* is another. The semicolon follows the first clause followed by the conjunctive adverb *however* and a comma that links both clauses.

A third major use of the semicolon is between items in a series when there is internal punctuation.

> Literature books are often divided by genres: novels, with an excerpt or two; short stories, which vary in length; drama, with parts of scenes and parts of acts; and poetry, which may range from the classic to the modern.

• Remember:

Do not use a semicolon to separate a subordinate clause from the rest of the sentence.

Without semicolons the reader would have to mentally sort out the major divisions. Semicolons help the writer help the reader.

Commas (,)

The comma comes from the Greek *komma*, which means "stamp." It is the symbol most frequently used in modern English to separate ideas or elements within a sentence. Interestingly, the comma is a vertical abbreviation of the virgule (/) that simply became shorter and shorter throughout its history until it morphed into a dot with a tail.

In our *Acts of Teaching* (second edition) we have the four major uses of the comma explained and delineated. Most grammar books list at least a dozen comma rules, several exceptions, and almost as many "do not" cautions; therefore, commas overwhelm us and we resort to the "salt and pepper" method of sprinkling them in a text by the seat of our pants. In truth commas are meant to help readers, not bedevil writers.

> If we cook Jacob will eat everything.

Obviously, unless the writer is playing some joke using Jonathan Swift's *A Modest Proposal,* the intention is not to cook Jacob. The simple comma placed after the word *cook* will clarify the correct intention. And that is the bottom line reason for commas—to prevent misreading.

> If we cook, Jacob will eat everything.

This is a grammar book after all, so we are listing the major uses for commas—not to overwhelm but for the sake of thoroughness.

- To separate items in a series, including the use of the "serial comma" sometimes called the "Oxford comma," which is the last comma—the one used between the *and* and the preceding word—for total clarity.

> I love cherries, watermelon, bananas, and peaches.

- To connect two independent clauses using coordinating conjunctions.

> Sophia loves to travel, but her husband is a stay-at-home guy.

- To set off long introductory elements in a sentence.

> After preparing enough tamales for three families, Abuela rested in her favorite rocking chair.

- To set off nonrestrictive (grammatically unnecessary to the essential meaning of the sentence) information, including appositives.

> Henrietta, the bratty girl down the street, plays tricks on the little kids.

- To set off an addressed person's name.

> Dr. Hamilton, can you tell me what is wrong with me?

- To separate dates and address—in addresses a comma follows every item after the first.

> Please come to 14 Pine Avenue, Moosetown, Texas, on September 1, 2009.

- After the salutation of a friendly letter and before the signature of any letter.

> Dear Mom,

> Love, Arnie

- To set off titles or degrees following a proper name.

> Marion Lusky, Ph.D., H.L.D.

- No comma is used between a last name and the Roman numeral that designates generations.

> Arthur Pertile III

- Most sources agree that the comma between the surname and *Jr.* or *Sr.* is optional.

> Raymond Miklos, Jr.

Raymond Miklos Sr.

- To set off a direct quotation.

"No, I never told David that," protested Jim.

- To separate coordinate adjectives not joined by *and*.

We want to extend one caution: do not use a comma to join two independent clauses. That is called a comma splice. The comma is the weakest punctuation mark and quite simply is not strong enough to bind together two powerful independent clauses.

Coordinate and Cumulative Adjectives

People always ask us some variation of this question: "How does that rule about commas and adjectives before a noun work?" The answer depends upon whether the adjectives are coordinate or cumulative.

Coordinate adjectives

If the adjectives are coordinate, that is, equal in modifying the noun, use a comma.

Reynolds Price wrote *A Long and Happy Life*.

This title contains coordinate adjectives. Both *long* and *happy* equally modify the noun *life;* therefore, the title could read *A Long, Happy Life* or *A Happy, Long Life.* In other

• Remember:

Do not overuse commas. Some papers contain so much "salt and pepper" the commas do not clarify but distract the reader.

words if the *and* can be replaced with a comma or the comma with an *and* or if the words can be rearranged and still carry the same meaning, you have coordinate adjectives.

Cumulative adjectives

If the adjectives are cumulative, that is, they gather momentum by modifying each other in turn, we call them cumulative and use no comma. In Emily R. Grosholz's essay "On Necklaces," we find a perfect example of cumulative adjectives.

> . . .heavy round dark crushed-glass-coated oversize beads . . .

Beginning with the adjective closest to the noun *beads,* we see how each adjective modifies a larger word group. *Oversize* modifies *beads, crushed-glass-coated* modifies *oversize beads, dark* modifies *crushed-glass-coated oversize beads, round* modifies *dark crushed-glass-coated oversize beads,* and *heavy* modifies *round dark crushed-glass-coated oversize beads.* Notice we cannot insert the word *and* between cumulative adjectives without marring the rhetorical effect:

> *heavy and round and dark and crushed-glass-coated and oversized beads.*

Therefore, we do not insert commas. Nor can we rearrange the adjectives:

> *dark oversize heavy crushed-glass-coated round beads* without jarring the rules of the order of adjectives.

Apostrophes (')

We didn't have apostrophes until the printing press. Printers used these marks to show missing letters, and they still serve this function as grammatical contractions. Coming from the Greek *apostrophos,* which means "to turn away," the apostrophe quite literally turns away the letter, so it goes missing. It logically follows that Hart would label apostrophes "tourners."

In 1976, Roger McGough wrote "Apostrophe," a poem that succinctly captures the function of this mark:

> **Apostrophe**
> 'twould be nice to be
> an apostrophe
> floating above an s
> hovering like a paper kite
> in between the its
> eavesdropping, tiptoeing
> high above the thats
> an inky comet
> spiralling
> the highest tossed
> of hats
>
> "Apostrophe" from The Mersey Sound by Roger McGough
> (© Roger McGough [1967]) is reproduced by permission
> of PFG (www.pfd.co.uk) on behalf of Roger McGough.

Apostrophes show possession:

> *Daniel's car*

> *the girls' gymshorts*

- Remember:

An apostrophe with an *s* forms the plurals of lowercase letters (Cross all your *t's*.), but just an *s* is used for uppercase letters (The teacher decorated the room with capital *As* for the *Scarlet Letter.*), for numbers (During the *1950s*, girls wore crinoline slips under their skirts.), and symbols (Some people put three **s* in a row to show an omission.).

Hence they float "above an *s*." Apostrophes also indicate the letter missing in a contraction (*wasn't*) or the letters missing in dialects (*Mornin', Miss Ritz.*) Hence they hover "in between the its" or tiptoe "high above the thats."

Quotation marks (" ")

Quotation marks have a fascinating history, coming to us primarily from biblical texts. This special sign—the *diple*, meaning double, was used in the margin of the manuscript to draw attention to that particular part of the text. Printers eventually put them on the line then raised them above the text like inverted commas to indicate passages of direct speech; therefore, we have synonyms for them such as *inverted commas, quotes, speech marks, or turned double commas.* Dr. Kelley Barger, an early childhood professor, helps little children understand their function by calling them "little lips"—two lips (") to show when the direct speech starts and two lips (") to show when it ends.

For some reason, aside from the comma, no punctuation seems as confusing to writers as quotation marks. Here are the rules plain and simple:

1. Use quotation marks to enclose exact text.

> John Fredrick Nims says, "Mythology is a natural product of the symbolizing mind."

2. Enclose a person's spoken words in quotation marks.

> My lawyer said, "There is a hard way and an easy way to do this."

3. Use single quotation marks to enclose a quotation within a quotation.

> Leela, my saleslady, exclaimed, "Wait until you hear the latest from Ann Stordahl! 'I've updated my wardrobe with something red, a touch of leopard, and a great motorcycle jacket for weekends.'"

4. Use quotation marks around the titles of others' works.

> Ezra Pound's "In a Station of the Metro" remains my favorite two-line poem.

5. Use quotation marks to set off words or expressions used in a particular way.

> In 1551 John Hart called the colon "joint."

Punctuation with Quotation Marks

• Remember:

Do not put something in quotation marks for common slang or to be funny.

Commas and periods go inside the quotation marks.

There is only one exception. When citing something in academic writing, follow this model:

exact words go in quotation marks
source goes in parentheses
the period goes *outside* the closing parenthesis.

"The more experience students have in selecting an organizational structure, the more critical they become" (Carroll and Wilson, *Acts of Teaching*, 2008, 40).

Semicolons and colons go outside the closing quotation mark.

Question and exclamation marks go inside the closing quotation mark if they belong to the quotation, outside if they belong to the larger unit.

The teacher asked, "Did you begin with a global statement or 'iffy' question?"

> Did the teacher really ask you "How do you think it would change the play if Hamlet were a girl"?

Generally when a quotation is introduced or interrupted, use commas to show the separation.

> "When teaching," the professor said, "remember to show not tell."

When quoting long passages of several paragraphs, put the quotation marks at the beginning of each paragraph and at the end of the entire passage. With dialogue, indent anew for each speaker.

Hyphens (-)

The Greek *huph hen* was a diacritical mark used to indicate a compound word or two words meant to be read as one. Some early texts show a hyphen that looks more like an equal sign with two lines to show the two words (=). Today we have a simplified mark of one line most often used to indicate word division—a break at the end of a line and the parts of some compound words, most often when there are two or more adjectives before a noun

> friendly-looking dog.

Because of the trend to simplify language, some former hyphenations have become simple compounds (noncompliance). This is particularly interesting because in 1551 John Hart called hyphens "joiners."

• Remember:

Hyphenate all compound numbers from twenty-one through ninety-nine.

En dashes (—)

Technically the en dash—in traditional type the width of the letter *N*—is slightly larger than a hyphen and slightly smaller than an em dash. Besides word division, we use the en dash to

- separate elements in dates (2005–2009; 11–13–37)
- to show the termination of a date has not yet happened (2009–).

Em dashes (—)

Em dashes come to us from printing. The em dash is the width of the letter *M* in traditional type. The em dash serves five functions:

1. to show a lapse in thought or sentence structure

   Harry thought—if that is what he was doing—the class was over.

2. to set off appositives in a series

   The head cheerleader announced—Beth, Amy, and Maria—the finalists.

3. to precede explanations

   To make an A in that class is difficult—you really have to study. (The em dash used this way replaces words like *in other words* or *that is*.)

4. to show faltering speech

"*Si*—I mean yes," Mario stuttered.

5. to show an incomplete sentence (with no period) instead of ellipsis

When she saw the stranger behind the door, she—

Parentheses ( )

Parentheses, sometimes called round brackets, are marks that come from the Greek *parentithenai,* meaning "to insert." In the 14th century, parentheses were an alternative to commas for marking the inclusion of some grammatical unit in a sentence. Technically the marks are *parens* while what is inside is the *thesis,* but over time the marks themselves have come to be called parentheses.

The function of parentheses has not changed appreciably since the 14th century. Looking a bit like fences, parentheses are still used to enclose all manner of supplementary information:

John Hart called parentheses "closures."

• Remember:

Like the comma caution, do not overuse parentheses.

minor digressions

(Did I tell you Suzie got married?),

asides

(please don't repeat this),

references

(*Inspiring the Classics,* 26),

directions

(see chapter 2),

numbers after written numbers to ensure accuracy

($20),

numbers, letters, or enumerations that mark divisions in a text

(There are three reasons she quit: (1) she knew she was losing her memory, (2) she wanted too much time off, (3) she didn't get along with her co-workers.),

and the occasional question mark to designate questionable accuracy

(?).

Brackets [ ]

Brackets, sometimes called square brackets, are used primarily to insert something such as an explanation to text already in parentheses

(Over thirty obsolete punctuation marks have been identified in early manuscripts [through the work of linguists and anthropologists], most of them disappearing when the printing press appeared.),

to correct a mistake

> (Shakspre [Shakespeare]),

and to enclose

> [sic] to show that the mistake in a quotation is not the fault of the person quoting the quotation.

Braces { }

Braces enclose two or more lines of text or listed items to show that they are considered as a unit.

Ellipses (. . . or * * *)

Ellipses come from the Greek *elleipsis,* which means "to fall short." And that is exactly what ellipses indicate—some type of omission—such as words omitted from a quotation

> This quotation comes from Psalms XLVIII, 2: "Beautiful for situation, the joy of the whole earth is Mount Zion . . . the city of the great King."

• Remember:

If the omitted material comes at the end of the sentence, use the proper end punctuation after the ellipses mark.

Ellipses marks are three periods or asterisks with spaces in between.

> My mother never finished her favorite saying. We finished for her. "Do not count your chickens before they are . . .

> Lady Macbeth asks in Act II of *Macbeth,* "Is this a dagger which I see before me . . . ?"

Italics

The word *italics* comes from the Latin *italicus,* which referred to the sloping handwriting characteristic of that written

164 • Brushing Up on Grammar

in Italy during the ancient and medieval periods. With the advent of the computer and all its fonts, italics as a font has replaced underlining and is now considered a punctuation mark.

We italicize all long titles such as books

Steinbeck's *The Grapes of Wrath*

book length poems

Beowulf

films

The Godfather

musical productions

Handel's *Messiah*

and compositions

Gershwin's *Porgy and Bess*

works of art

Michelangelo's *David*

magazines

Redbook

TV shows

CSI New York

radio shows

NPR Morning Edition

ships

Titanic

spacecraft

Apollo VII

aircraft

Piper PA- -32R-301 Saratoga

trains

Silver Streak

and newspapers

The Houston Chronicle

If the *A, An,* or *The* appear before a newspaper or magazine in a sentence, these words are not italicized. (We read the *Houston Chronicle* every day.) Shorter works such as short stories, chapters in books, and poems are placed in quotation marks.

Foreign words and phrases such as

italicus

are placed in italics as are words referred to as words, letters referred to as letters, and numbers referred to as numbers.

Capital Letters

ometimes, feeling Hamlet-like, we are inclined to moan (with apologies to the Bard, of course):

> To cap or not to cap, that is the question:
>   Whether 'tis nobler in the mind to suffer
>   the slings and arrows of outrageous mistakes,
>   Or to take a reference book against a sea of capitals,
>   And by opposing end them?

We think this capitalization angst, this indecision we see among so many is a 17th-century linguistic residue. Then it was not only fashionable but also correct to capitalize not only the beginning of every sentence, proper names, titles, forms of address, and personified nouns but also *every noun!* Look at this excerpt from Jonathan Swift's *Baucis and Philemon* (1706):

> In antient [sic.] Time, as Story tells
> The Saints would often leave their Cells,
> And strode about, but hide their Quality,
> To try the People's Hospitality.

We find reading this a bit unnerving, so we were happy to learn that 18th-century grammarians corrected this overuse of caps. Still, we capitalize many words.

We capitalize:

- the first word in a sentence

> Will you come to the store with me?

- proper nouns and proper adjectives

> Mary visited the White House with Uncle Seth.

- months, holidays, and days of the week

> Today is Labor Day, a special Monday in September.

- school subjects if they are derived from countries or if a number or letter follows them

> She studied Spanish; he took Mathematics 104.

- the pronoun *I* and the vocative *O* or *Oh*

> I screamed, "Oh! it's a ghost."

- titles of books, magazines, musical compositions, programs, films, works of art

> Her favorite book and film is *Gone with the Wind*, but her favorite magazine is *Cosmopolitan*. His favorite musical composition is Verdi's *Aida*, but his favorite work of art is Van Gogh's *Starry, Starry Night*.

- the first word of a quoted sentence but not the first word of a quoted fragment

> She asked me, "Why don't you cut your hair?"

- all words in a quotation that were capitalized by the author

> Colleen Wainwright said, "Being friendless taught me how to be a friend. Funny how that works."

- abbreviations for departments and government agencies, organizations, corporations, trade names, and the call letters of radio and television stations

> I am speaking on WQET about my work with the SPCA.

- first, last, and all major words in titles

> Have you read *The Elements of Style* by Strunk and White?

- first word after a colon in a title

> Her speech is entitled "Reading and Writing: Lessons from the Brain."

- the second part of a hyphenated word in a title if it is as important as the first part

> Sue found the book *Anglo-Saxon People* fascinating.

- the first word following a colon if it is a formal statement

> The warning was posted on the castle door: Beware all who enter here.

- the first word of a statement or question inserted into a sentence without quotation marks

> The question remains, Did you do it?

- the first word and any noun in the salutation of a letter

> Dear Friends,

- the first word in the closing of a letter

> Yours truly,

- initials, titles, abbreviations of titles that precede proper names

> Dr. Walker is personable.

- academic degrees and their abbreviations

> Martin earned his Doctor of Philosophy degree so now he can write Ph.D. after his name.

- geographical names but not *north, south, east, west* when these words indicate direction.

> I had trouble with north, east, west, and south when I lived in South Carolina.

- buildings, brand names, ships, planes, railways, airlines

> The Empire State Building stands tall in New York City.

- historical periods, events, documents, and political parties

> Henrietta took a course that covered two major historical periods: The Salem Witch Trials and The McCarthy Witch Hunts.

- religions, races, denominations, and nationalities

> Doris was Catholic, but her Scottish husband was Lutheran.

- names of a specific deity, sections of the Bible, and sacred books

> My five-year-old cousin informed me that the New Testament is all about Jesus.

- names (except *page*) that are followed by numerals or letters

> Harold looked in his guidebook on page 104 for the location of Station 12.

- all languages

> Much to our surprise, Ana spoke three languages: English, Spanish, and Filipino.

- copyrighted games

> We bought his sister Monopoly for Christmas.

- brand names

> In cosmetics I like Chanel, but for skin care nothing beats La Prairie.

- personified nouns, epithets that substitute for a person's name or title, and nicknames

> The Kingston Trio had a hit "Be Still My Heart," and in the lyrics they call the wind Mariah.

- streets, boulevards, avenues, and other road names

> We live on West State Road just east of the railroad tracks.

• Remember:

Some folks are "CAP HAPPY." They use, or rather misuse, capital letters to show force. Actually a woman was fired recently from her position for being "CAP HAPPY" in her e-mails. Apparently her e-mails were too "shouty." So remember, don't be "CAP HAPPY" and don't be "shouty" in writing.

Teaching Punctuation: Three Ideas

People always ask us where we get our ideas and we always answer, "From books!" We don't mean idea books; we mean storybooks, picture books, graphic novels—all kinds of books. In this case, Robin Pulver's delightful children's book *Punctuation Takes a Vacation* coupled with John Hart's 1551 book mentioned repeatedly throughout this section, gave us the perfect way to teach punctuation.

1. Students research the various marks, the history of their names, and their functions. Then based on that inquiry, they rename each mark, present a justification, and give an example. For example, Hart called the question mark the "asker"; Pulver has quotation marks signing their postcard "The Yack-ity Yaks." Because the brain loves a challenge, this way into punctuation is both fun and fruitful. After all, to move information from the short-term memory to the long-term memory, we have to work it. Through this strategy of applying their knowledge, students are indeed working those sometimes-illusive marks into their long-term memories.

2. Another idea is to use Mr. Stops. Students research the punctuation marks, including their history. Give a copy of Mr. Stops to each student or to a group of students and invite them

to find all the punctuation marks they can find. Through this "Where's Waldo" approach, students revel in the challenge, especially in groups.

Conclude by making a copy of Mr. Stops for the overhead or document camera and mark the answers from the students. This produces lively discussion and allows students to apply their research as they justify their answers.

3. The third idea is to give students sentences without punctuation (they abound on the Internet) and enjoy the results. Here are a few.

James called John come here

Don't scratch Sally cried Tom

I want to invite Billy Bob and Austin

Mrs. Burns the teacher is absent

Give me twenty five dollar bills

Mary Queen of Scots wept bitterly an hour after she was beheaded

Caesar entered on his head his helmet on his feet his sandals in his hand his sword on his forehead a frown and sat down

(See also *Acts*, 2008, 93−102 for more ideas on punctuation.)

MAKING IT WORK:

RATIOCINATION—GRAMMAR WITHIN THE WRITING PROCESS

We now get to the point in grammar where we make it work, make it work within the writing process—where we get it all together. We can remember returning from graduate school filled with missionary zeal, intoning in all our workshops, "Teach grammar within the writing process." Teachers nodded their heads in agreement but went back to six weeks of grammar, six weeks of composition, and then on to their beloved literature. Finally, at one large state convention as we again intoned, "Teach grammar within the writing process," a brave teacher raised her hand and said, "I think most of us believe that is best but how do we do that?"

What an eye-opener! For years as a discipline, we had separated grammar and writing, expecting the students to make the connections perhaps because we ourselves didn't have a clear method for teaching grammar, composition, and literature together. This set us to researching and working with students to develop a method that would work. The result was a seminal article.

In 1982 Carroll wrote and *English Journal* published that article, "Ratiocination and Revision or Clues in the Written Draft." Carroll placed its thesis—teach grammar within the writing process—squarely during revising and made the case for how ratiocination taps higher-level thinking skills. Subsequently the article was included in both editions of *Acts of Teaching.*

Teachers who know about grammar and who understand the research, teachers who teach and who do not merely assign and assess, have had remarkable success with their students learning grammar, doing real revision, and experimenting with the craft using this approach. As one teacher told us, "My kids like grammar now. They are involved, and I can teach all the grammar in my curriculum guide for my grade level just by having them circle those 'to be' verbs."

What Is Ratiocination?

Pure and simple, ratiocination presents teachers with a concrete way to teach grammar within the writing process and presents students with a concrete way to apply grammar to their writing to improve their writing. Based on years of brain and cognitive developmental research, this act of inviting students to re-enter their writing to make it better is a hybrid of the writing as a mode of learning theories of Janet Emig, Lev Vygotsky, A. R. Luria, and Jerome Bruner; the sentence combining strategies of William Strong; the learn-by-doing philosophy of John Dewey; the stimulate and guide the self-development of students philosophy of Alfred North Whitehead; the "abstract truth made tangible" balloons of S.W. Clark; the visualizing diagramming techniques of Reed and Kellogg; and our joint collective experience of over eight decades of teaching.

The Procedure

Because this is a hands-on, student-centered, higher-level strategy, students need markers to color code their drafts. On a large sheet of butcher paper, one that can be saved, stored, and resurrected as needed, the teacher makes three columns. Students do the same in their writing notebooks, using the left page for the first two columns and the facing page for the third column.

Everyone labels the first column *Code,* the second column *Clue,* and the third column *Decode.* By giving the students a code and a clue, they have a specific reason to re-enter their papers *during the process.*

For the purposes of this book, we are taking one code through several grade levels. Under *code* everyone draws a circle in red. Under *clue* everyone writes the clue—in this case—*verbs.* Now the work begins. Teachers may do as few or as many of these decodes as grade level, mastery, attention, and the curricular mandates allow. Teachers tackle the grammar concepts during the decoding and students immediately implement them in their writing. Circling verbs as a starter allows teaching everything from (obviously) verbs, active and passive, tenses, voice, and all things related to verbs plus subject/verb agreement, participles, subject complements, direct and indirect objects, fragments, weak repetition, word choice, vocabulary—well, the works. Everything hinges on verbs.

Five Student Samples

Second grade

For second grade, after the students circled their verbs, the teacher shared the following decodes, which she phrased as questions. She explained that her curriculum introduces "to be" verbs at the beginning of second grade and that they had played "Simple Simon" to solidify the difference between active verbs and verbs of existence. Because they also work on vocabulary, she uses ratiocination to call attention to words for the students to reconsider. So in January, she shared two major decodes:

> • Can you make any verbs say more exactly what you mean?
> • Do you have any "to be" verbs? Can you make them stronger?

Everyone herd the rumbling of Tyrannosarus rex! Everyone ran, and ran.
He almost got them but they were
to quick. So after Tyrannosaurus
rex left they had a meeting
at Duckbill's house.

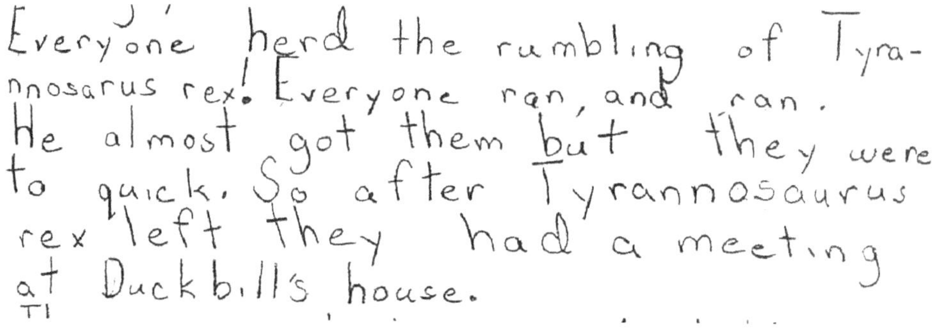

fig. 10.1

Everyone herd the rumbling of Tyrannosarus rex!
Everyone ran, and ran. He almost got them but they
were to quick. So after Tyrannosaurus rex left they
had a meeting at Duckbill's house.

At first Aileen circled *herd, ran, ran, got, were.* The
teacher, who hunkers down by the children as they work,
nudged Aileen through thoughtful questions. "What did Tyrannosaurus rex do after all the others ran and ran?"

Aileen said, "He left."
"That doing word shows action, doesn't it?"
"Oh, it's a verb!" Aileen almost shouted.
"Now let's look at what all the other dinosaurs did after
    Tyrannosaurus rex left?"
"They had a meeting."
"*Had* is what we call an irregular verb, Aileen. It goes like
    this: *have, had, had.* You used the past tense of *have* and
    you used it correctly, but you forgot to circle it. Why
    don't you circle it now? And, by the way, Aileen, the
    herd you circled is really a noun—like a herd of
    sheep—remember when we studied homophones? *H e r d*
    and *h e a r d* are homophones. *Heard* is a verb and has
    the little word *ear* in it because it shows the action of lis-
    tening. It means to hear with your ears. Both words have
    the same sound but they are spelled differently and have
    different meanings. Which one do you mean here?"

Aileen quickly said, "The one with the ear in it."

"Then let's use that verb, Aileen. Now get busy ratiocinating your verbs. You did a good job here."

We let Aileen work and then looked at what she had done. *Herd* became *heard*. She changed *got* to *stomped* and *were* to *ran*. Impressed, we talked to Aileen. She told us she loved "ratiocinating because she got to use better words." When we talked to the teacher, she told us she noted that most of the students needed some work on those commas before *and*. "They still have pseudo-concepts," she said. "When they see *and*, they put a comma." She also mentioned they needed a reteach on *to, too, two*. We complimented the fact that Aileen corrected the second spelling of Tyrannosaurus rex all by herself, without any nudging or help. The teacher, smiled and said, "I work hard on getting the kids to check and double check those kinds of words from the original reference."

Implications of Aileen's ratiocinating

Aileen's hard-working teacher knew her pedagogy. She didn't overwhelm her second graders, but challenged them. Allowing ownership, she didn't tell them what to do, she nudged and probed and allowed them the learning. She held them responsible for what she taught and made notes for future lessons. This is grammar in action, grammar within the writing process, grammar minus mindless worksheets. And the children loved it.

Fourth grade

Moving to fourth grade, we asked the teacher to tell us how she handles ratiocination. She told us that her kids love to write but hate to rewrite, so she just stays with the "to be" verbs, which she told us they overuse. "They love to see their writing grow on the page," she said, "but they are lazy in their excitement and don't really think about word choice. So I am hammering away at that through the 'to be' verbs." She also emphasizes tenses in her teaching. "We made those tense time lines."

For her decoding, she listed:

- change the "to be" verb to a livelier verb if you can
- combine sentences to get rid of "to be" verbs
- make sure you have a verb in every sentence
- do not change the "to be" verb in a quote or dialogue
- make sure your tenses are correct; check your tense time line

Fourth-grade sample

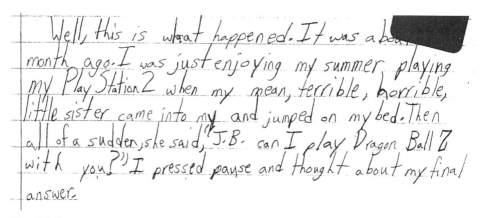

fig. 10.2

Well, this is what happened. It was about a month ago. I was just enjoying my summer, playing my Play Station 2 when my mean, terrible, horrible, little sister came into my . . . and jumped on my bed. Then all of a sudden, she said, "J.B. can I play Dragon Ball Z with you?" I pressed pause and thought about my final answer.

J.B. circled *is, was, was enjoying, playing, came, jumped, said, pressed, thought.*

J.B. noticed immediately that most of his verbs were in the past tense except *is* and *playing.* He fretted about that and finally decided to combine the first, second, and third sentences. He asked his teacher if he could do that. She asked, "What do you have in mind, J.B?"

"Well, I think I could get all those verbs in the past tense and get rid of the *is,*" he said.

"That might be fabulous, J.B. Work on it."

So he did. Finally writing

> *About a month ago I was enjoying my summer and was playing my Play Station 2 when my mean, terrible, horrible little sister came into my bedroom and jumped on my bed.*

When we talked to him, he told us proudly that he got rid of the *is.* We asked about *was enjoying* and *was playing.* He chewed on the eraser at the end of his pencil for a while before saying, "We learned that means the action was still going on. I was still playing my game and enjoying my summer vacation when the pest barged in." We suppressed a smile and noted the not-so-vague allusion to Judith Viorst's *Alexander and the Terrible, Horrible, No Good, Very Bad Day.*

We asked J.B. what he thought about ratiocinating. "It's cool," came the reply.

Implications of J.B.'s ratiocinating

Most impressive was J.B.'s willingness to reconstruct several sentences, especially since his teacher said that generally the students dislike rewriting. That J.B. totally dropped his first sentence (something students of this age don't usually do), combined the next two sentences, and changed his second sentence to an introductory phrase told us that J.B. was a compositional risk-taker even though he checked out the possibility with his teacher and got the go-ahead. It also told us that the teacher encouraged the students to manipulate their writing and ratiocination fit directly into that.

Seventh grade

When we move to middle school, we often see more extensive than reflexive writing, so the pieces become more stilted until these adolescents find their writing sea legs. Striving writers, lacking many rich writing environments or those who have been fed a steady diet of worksheets, tend to grab at "to be" verbs, giving little thought to other possibilities. Caesar typifies this. His teacher, introducing ratiocination to her seventh graders, most of whom had never experienced this strategy, worked totally with "to be" verbs. Her decoding list gave Caesar and his classmates choices for perhaps the first time.

- leave the "to be" verb because to change it would change the meaning
- change the "to be" verb to make the writing better, more precise
- if the "to be" verb signals a weak sentence, rework the sentence

The teacher explained each of the three decodes, gave examples from mentor texts, and then showed her circled verbs on the overhead. Together they ratiocinated the paper, changing her "to be" verbs according to the decoding suggestions.

Seventh-grade sample

Many people in gangs are usually middle school to high school students. Many of these students are influenced by an older friend, or relative who is in a gang. Why do people get in gangs? No one knows for sure, but some may get in gangs because they may have problems at home, or they do it to get back at their parents. Some people were in gangs, but then realized it wasn't worth it. Some people get rolled out, but some are found dead, and dumped on the streets!

fig. 10.3

Many people in gangs are usually middle school to high school students. Many of these people are influenced by an old friend, or relative who is in a gang. Why do people get in gangs? No one knows for sure, but some may get in gangs because they may have problems at home, or they do it to get back at their parents. Some people were in gangs, but then realized it wasn't worth it. Some people get rolled out, but some are found dead, and dumped on the streets!

Caesar circled *are, are influenced, is, get, get, have, do, get back, were, wasn't, get, are found, dumped.*

After the lesson on ratiocinating and the model, the students set to work. Caesar struggled. The newness of changing verbs or reworking sentences stymied him. His teacher, walking around the room and helping the students, eventually arrived at his desk.

"I can't do this," Caesar flatly announced.

"Sure you can, *mi hijo*. Let's take a look." Wisely she skipped to *is*. "Let's see if we can think of another word that is more precise, that says what you mean here. When we say someone is *in* a gang, what is another way we can say that, a way that shows ownership in the gang?"

A master of wait time, this teacher gave Caesar plenty of time to think. Finally, almost in a whisper, Caesar offered, "belonged to." His teacher rewarded him a high five, more words of encouragement, and then moved on. As she did, she tossed over her shoulder, "And I like the way you wrote 'get rolled out.' That really works there."

Caesar smiled. Then he re-entered his paper. When we checked with him at the end of the period, this is what we read:

> Usually middle school and high school students belong to gangs. Many of these students are influenced by an older friend, or relative who belongs to a gang. Why do people join? No one knows for sure, but some may join because they have problems at home, or they want to get back at their parents. Some were in gangs, but then realized it wasn't worth it. Some roll out, some die, some get dumped on the streets!

Implications of Caesar's ratiocinating

Perhaps the most telling thing about Caesar's experience with ratiocination rises up as the ownership he took for his writing. Once encouraged after working with his teacher, he dared to rearrange the opening of this excerpt, replacing the *are* with *belong*. On his own he decided *join* replaced *get in* more precisely in two places—a revision for the better. While he did nothing to change the next to the last sentence, he surprised us all with that beautiful parallelism in his last sentence. When he shared his revision, his teacher jumped on that, wrote it on the board, and used it as a mini-teach on parallel construction. Caesar radiated with pride.

Tenth grade

When we visited this tenth grade in mid-September, the class had already taken a paper through the process. We saw Edmondo's prewriting and rough draft stapled behind his final paper. Interestingly he wrote possible titles this way and that all over the top margin of one of his earlier drafts: "Hunt of a Lifetime," "Sacrificed Prey," "The Thrill of the Hunt," "Long Ago," "Days Not Forgotten." He abandoned all of these for "On the Hunt."

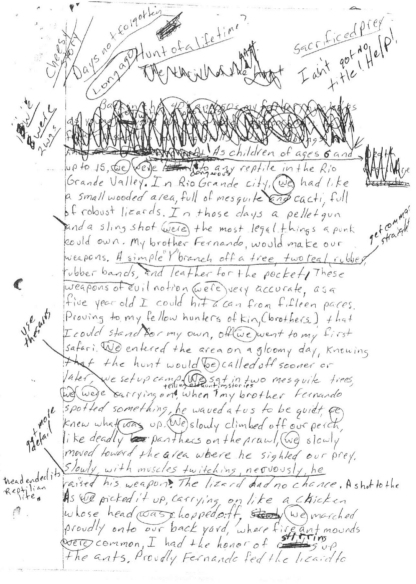

fig. 10.4

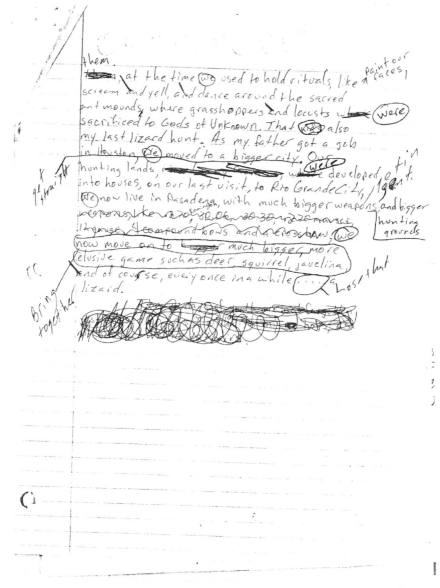

them.

at the time we used to hold rituals, like paint our faces,
scream and yell, and dance around the sacred
ant mounds, where grasshoppers and locusts were
sacrificed to Gods of Unknown. That was also
my last lizard hunt. As my father got a job
in Houston, we moved to a bigger city. Our
hunting lands, were developed
into houses, on our last visit, to Rio Grande City, 19
We now live in Pasadena, with much bigger weapons and bigger
weapons like a 20.06, 30.30, remmington
12 gauge, compound bows and crossbow. We hunting grounds
now move on to much bigger, more
elusive game such as deer, squirrel, javelina
and of course, every once in a while a lizard.
lizard.

Bring together

fig. 10.5

    The teacher explained that her students had been ratiocinating since middle school and automatically circled their "to be" verbs. Still they often opted for the easily accessible "to be" verb rather than the more precise verb. While their writing had grown in sophistication compared to middle schoolers, she decided at least in September to continue work on changing those "to be" verbs to livelier verbs but with a twist. That was her major decode for this paper. Here is what she wrote under the decode column on her butcher paper:

To consider removing "to be" verbs in your writing, try to
- combine sentences for variety of length
- begin with an introductory phrase or a subordinate clause
- change a sentence to a clause and add it to the previous sentence

These decodes gave the teacher the opportunity to teach various ways to combine sentences, including proper punctuation marks. She also taught introductory phrases, subordinate clauses, and independent clauses.

Tenth-grade sample

"On the Hunt"

Long ago my father introduced hunting to his three oldest sons. As they became accustomed to the skill, I was in the house watching Sesame Street. Then my day came, I was ~~taken~~ lifted up from my big bird chair, and placed in the wilderness. Across the street, there was a big lot full of weeds and trees. Then my days of hunting were numbered. As children of ages of 5 to 13, my brothers and I were public enemies to any reptile in the Rio Grande Valley. In Rio Grande City, our home town, people knew us as "the Punks." We owned simple weapons of destruction—a pellet gun, and a slingshot. My brother Fernando would make our slingshots.

fig. 10.6

> Long ago my father introduced hunting to his three old-
> est sons. As they became accustomed to the skill, I was
> in the house watching Sesame Street. Then my day
> came. I was lifted up from my big bird chair and placed
> in the wilderness. Across the street, there was a big lot
> full of weeds and trees. Then my days of hunting were
> numbered. As children of ages of 5 to 13, my brothers
> and I were public enemies to any reptile in the Rio
> Grande Valley. In Rio Grande City, our hometown,
> people knew us as "The Punks." We owned simple
> weapons of destruction—a pellet gun, and a slingshot.

Instructed to circle the "to be" verbs, Edmondo circled *was,
was lifted, was, were, were.* His other verbs such as *placed, knew,
owned* showed an internalizing of the concept of striving toward the
best verb. Although challenged to rid the paper of half the "to be"
verbs, Edmondo decided to get rid of all of them, which he did.

Following the decoding suggestions, Edmondo first changed *I
was lifted up from my big bird chair and placed in the wilderness* to
an introductory dependent, subordinate clause. He totally rewrote
(some of which appeared in an earlier draft) *Across the street, there
was a big lot full of weeds and trees* and combined his rewrite with
the introductory dependent clause. Reworking *Then my days of
hunting were numbered* to read *I was hooked,* he tacked that independent clause onto the dependent clause to form a sophisticated
syntactically mature sentence. In other words, Edmondo followed
the decoding suggestions and made his paper significantly better.

> Long ago my father introduced hunting to his three old-
> est sons. As they became accustomed to the skill, I sat in
> the house watching Sesame Street. Then my day came.
> After Dad lifted me up from my big bird chair and
> placed me in the wilderness of the wooded area across
> the street full of mesquite and cacti and robust lizards, I
> was hooked. As children ages 5 to 13, my brothers and I
> roamed the lot as public enemies to any reptile in the Rio
> Grande Valley. In Rio Grande City, our hometown, peo-
> ple knew us as "The Punks." We owned simple weapons
> of destruction—a pellet gun, and a slingshot.

Implications of Edmondo's ratiocinating

Already a pretty good little writer with an eye for detail and drama, Edmondo grew through the ratiocination of this paper because of his ability to manipulate those clauses to work for him. He quickly caught on to dependent clauses because his teacher worked with the AAAs, BBs, TUTU, IS, and WWWWWWs mnemonic device with the students. This simple strategy helped Edmondo deal with some weak sentences and strengthen his paper. When we interviewed him, he said, "At first it was just a cheesy story, but now I like it."

Eleventh grade

Christine, an English III AP and Honors student, wrote beautifully, owned an extensive vocabulary, and worked revision like a pro. Her teacher, proud of her, showed us her working drafts on a paper entitled "In Search of the Golden Median of Morality." To prove her virtuosity with language, we present drafts of one of the paragraphs in the paper as well as her struggle with her final paragraph in her final draft.

This is Christine's trial rough draft:

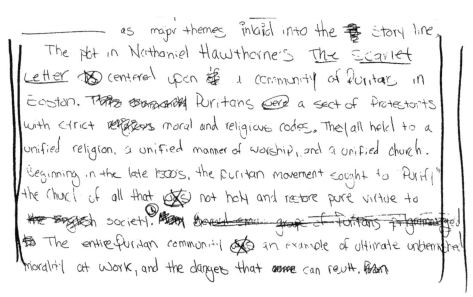

fig. 10.7

The plot in Nathaniel Hawthorne's The Scarlet Letter centered upon a community of Puritans in Boston. Puritans were a sect of Protestants with strict moral and religious codes. They all held to a unified religion, a unified manner of worship, and a unified church. Beginning in the late 1500's, the Puritan movement sought to "purify" the church of all that not holy and restore pure virture to the English society.[1] The entire Puritan community an example of ultimate unblemished morality at work, and the dangers that can result.

Here we see Christine already striking out some of her "to be" verbs and disregarding several sentence beginnings. Her writing is sloppy but coded with lines and numbers, but her craft already shows. Look at the nice parallel structure of "They all held to a unified religion, a unified manner of worship, and a unified church." On a separate page, she had the following written:

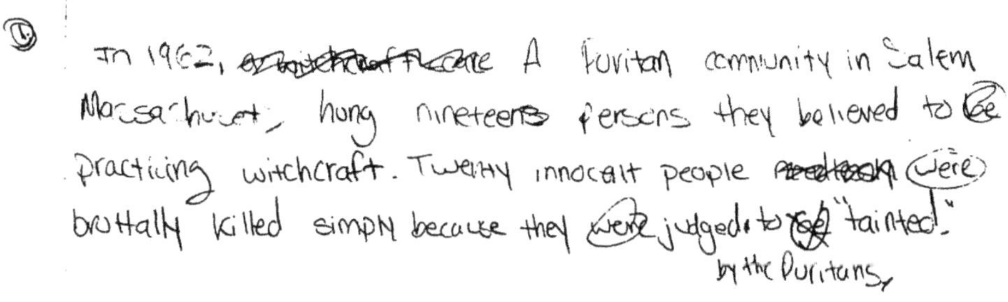
① In 1962, A Puritan community in Salem Massachuset hung nineteen persons they believed to be practicing witchcraft. Twenty innocent people were bruttally killed simply because they were judged to be "tainted." by the Puritans,

fig. 10.8

In 1962, A Puritan community in Salem Massachusets hung nineteen persons they believed to be practicing witchcraft. Twenty innocent people were bruttally killed simply because they were judged to "tainted."
by the Puritans

In her rough draft, Christine continues to pay attention to her "to be" verbs, she miswrites 1962 for 1592, has some spelling errors, but she revises as she writes and decides to add a prepositional phrase, which clarifies. At this point she doesn't seem to notice the discrepancy between nineteen and twenty persons.

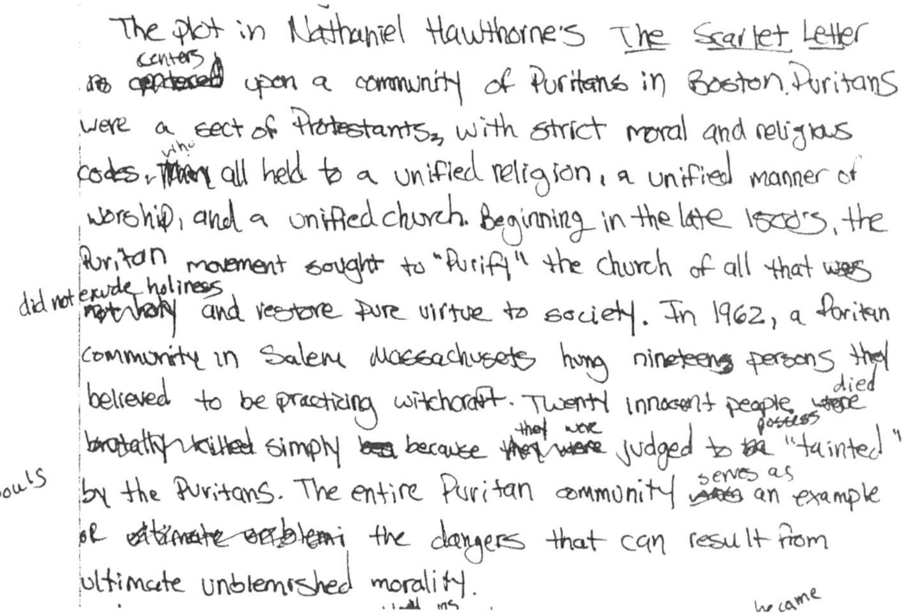
The plot in Nathaniel Hawthorne's The Scarlet Letter centers upon a community of Puritans in Boston. Puritans were a sect of Protestants, with strict moral and religious codes, who all held to a unified religion, a unified manner of worship, and a unified church. Beginning in the late 1500's, the Puritan movement sought to "Purify" the church of all that did not exude holiness and restore pure virtue to society. In 1962, a Puritan community in Salem Massachusets hung nineteen persons they believed to be practicing witchcraft. Twenty innocent people died simply because they were judged to possess "tainted" souls by the Puritans. The entire Puritan community serves as an example of the dangers that can result from ultimate unblemished morality.

fig. 10.9

> The plot in Nathaniel Hawthorne's <u>The Scarlet Letter</u> centers upon a community of Puritans in Boston. Puritans were a sect of Protestants with strict moral and religious codes, who all held to a unified religion, a unified manner of worship, and a unified church. Beginning in the late 1500's, the Puritan movement sought to "purify" the church of all that did not exude holiness and restore pure virtue to society. In 1962, a Puritan community in Salem Massachusets hung nineteen persons they believed to be practicing witchcraft. Twenty innocent people died simply because they were judged to posses "tainted" [in margin] souls by the Puritans. The entire Puritan community serves as an example of the dangers that can result from ultimate unblemished morality.

In this draft Christine revises much, doing so for the better: *centers* is more direct than *is centered,* she combines the second and third sentences by making the second a relative clause, she replaces *was not holy* with the impressive *did not exude holiness,* *were* with *died,* and we see her mind at work when she finally omits *brutally*—now spelled correctly—*killed,* as she considers *they were* and then decides to keep it, changes *to be* to *to possess,* adds the powerful imagistic word *souls,* and toys with exactly where to place *ultimate unblemished.* While she hasn't caught 1962 nor the incorrect spelling of Massachusetts and seems oblivious to the nineteen and twenty discrepancy, her work illustrates what fine teaching and ratiocination can do for a student writer.

Christine's next draft shows some math in the margin as she corrects the 1962 error. In the typing of it she had a typo *beggining,* which she corrected. Both corrections indicate a student who has been trained to reread her paper.

The final draft

Christine's teacher unhappily showed us her final paragraph in her "final draft." Claiming disappointment with what he perceived as "his class not concluding their papers with the same quality as the rest of their work," he initiated our advanced level of ratiocination. Motivated as they were, they rose to his challenge. Here are the clues he wrote under "Decoding" on his butcher paper. As he introduced each decode, he taught (or retaught) the concept and gave at least one example. He explained how in extensive papers, it is easy to fall back upon the quick "to be" verb.

- Continue trying to change "to be" verbs to active verbs.

  > *The Great Gatsby was about the frivolous society in America in the 20s.*

  > *The Great Gatsby's plot involved the frivolous society in America in the 20s.*

- Try not to start a sentence with the anticipatory subject *It* as in *It was, It is.* Your reader doesn't know the referent for the *it.*

> *It was a dark and stormy night.*

> *Dark and stormy, the night rolled in like black velvet covering everything.*

- If the subject is repeated in two consecutive sentences, one with a "to be" verb, delete it, drop one subject, and combine the sentences. Here the teacher offered these examples and as he did, he taught them the concept:

> *Jennifer accepted the award. Jennifer was overcome with emotion.*

> *Jennifer, overcome with emotion, accepted the award.*

or

> *Overcome with emotion, Jennifer accepted the award.*

- Even if there is no "to be" verb in one of two sentences, try changing the main verb of the subordinating sentence to its *-ing* participle form and combine the sentences. These were his examples:

> *Jennifer ran out of the auditorium. She waved her hands and gave the high five.*

> *Jennifer ran out of the auditorium, waving her hands and giving the high five.*

- If there is a "possessive" relationship between two sentences, use possessive pronouns (my, your, his, her, its, our, their, whose) to indicate the relationship between the subjects and change the verbs to participles.

> *The dog attacked the thief. The dog had bared teeth.*

Applying that decode, the teacher shared this example:

> *Baring his teeth, the dog attacked the thief.*

> *The dog, baring his teeth, attacked the thief.*

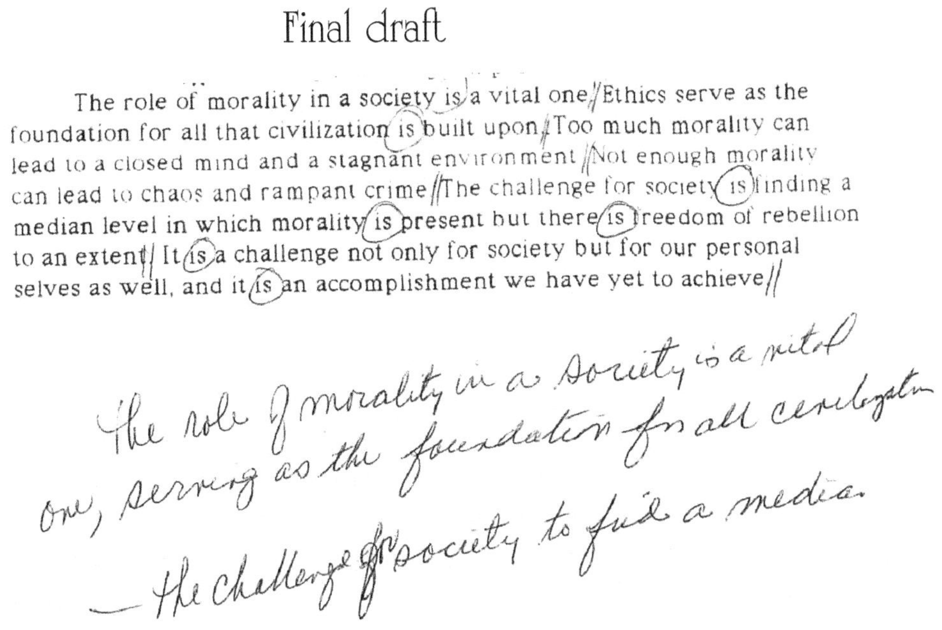

Final draft

The role of morality in a society is a vital one. Ethics serve as the foundation for all that civilization is built upon. Too much morality can lead to a closed mind and a stagnant environment. Not enough morality can lead to chaos and rampant crime. The challenge for society is finding a median level in which morality is present but there is freedom of rebellion to an extent. It is a challenge not only for society but for our personal selves as well, and it is an accomplishment we have yet to achieve.

The role of morality in a society is a vital one, serving as the foundation for all civilization

— the challenge of society to find a media

fig. 10.10

Dutifully Christine re-entered her paper once again, aghast that she had seven "to be" verbs in six sentences. Although they were not underlining their papers in alternate colors to test sentence length, she whispered to her friend, "Some of my sentences are choppy. Bummer."

After applying the ratiocination decodes, Christine ended her typed final paper with sophistication:

> The role of morality in society is a vital one, serving as its foundation for all civil acts. Too much morality leads to closed minds and stagnant environments but not enough morality leads to chaos and rampant crime. Society's challenge is to find a median level between morality and the freedom to rebel. Challenging individuals as well as society as a whole, we have yet to achieve that balance.

Implications of Christine's ratiocinating

Much to the delight of her teacher, Christine followed the decoding suggestion for the possessive relationship and greatly enhanced the opening of her final paragraph. She tapped her penchant for the parallel structure we saw in an earlier portion of her paper by setting up a thesis/antithesis construction in her second sentence; this is so important for AP and honor students. By changing the prepositional phrase *for society* to *Society's challenge,* Christine not only tightened her writing but also set up the coherence and unity of her powerful close.

Conclusion

Applicable at every level, as we see from these five student samples, ratiocination empowers student writers from the neophyte second grader to the sophisticated eleventh grader. Simply distributing worksheets or assigning exercises does not yield these results. We learn to write by writing. But students need both direct instruction and guided practice. They need to see models from the teacher's writing, from their peers, and from mentor texts. (Teachers confide that often students come up, book in hand, saying, "Look, I found another example of what you showed us yesterday in ratiocination.") Most of all students need the clues, the patience, the mentoring, and the flat out day-after-day teaching to enable them to re-enter their own writing, grapple with language, manipulate words, until, like the fighter imagery used so often by Ernest Hemmingway, they knock their meaning onto the page with powerful punches.

An added bonus of ratiocination is how it helps students on tests. So often they are required to choose the best from four possible rewrites. Often they are asked to proofread a passage as evidence that they know their grammar in context.

The following released state-mandated test excerpted examples, one from an elementary level test and one from a high school level test, bear this out. In both the students are given a passage to revise and edit. (These were copied exactly as they appeared on the test.)

Elementary level test excerpt

A Fun Collection

(1) I've been having fun starting a collection of the new state quarters. (2) Last week I bought a kit to help me with this project. (3) It has a cardboard holder for all 50 quarters and a book that tells about each quarter and the state it represents.

(4) I learned that it began in 1999 and will continue for 10 years. (5) The U.S. mint makes these quarters because it is the place where all our coins are made. (6) Each year the U.S. Mint produces quarters for only five states. (7) The Mint is making quarters in the same order that the states joined the United States. (8) I'll have to wait until 2004 to add the Texas quarter to my collection.

(9) My mom and me are both involved in collecting the state quarters.. . .

1. The meaning of sentence 4 can be improved by changing *it* to

   A. the cardboard holder

   B. my collection

   C. the book

   D. the state quarters program

2. What change, if any, should be made in sentence 5?

   A. Change *has* to **had**

   B. Change *it's* to **its**

   C. Change *special* to **speshal**

   D. Make no change

3. What change, if any, should be made in sentence 10?

   A. Change *mom* to **Mom**

   B. Change *me* to **I**

C. Change *are* to **is**

D. Make no change

High school level test excerpt

The American Red Cross

(1) The American Red Cross is an organization that aids people all around the world. (2) It started as a result of the efforts of a dedicated woman. (3) That woman was named Clara Barton. (4) It was during the Civil War that Barton began the work that lead to the establishment of the American Red Cross. (5) She assisted on the battlefield by nursing injured soldiers and helping transport supplies. (6) Eventually the Government of the United States selected her to serve as superintendent of nurses for the army.

1. What is the most effective way to combine sentences 2 and 3?

    A. It started as a result of the efforts of a dedicated woman, that woman was name Clara Barton.

    B. It started as a result of the efforts of a woman who was dedicated and named Clara Barton.

    C. It started as a result of the efforts of a dedicated woman named Clara Barton.

    D. It started as a result of the efforts of a dedicated woman she was named Clara Barton.

2. What change, if any, should be made in sentence 4?

    1. Change **was** to **is**

    2. Insert a comma after Civil War

    3. Change **lead** to **led**

    4. Make no change

3. What change, if any, should be made in sentence 6?

    A. Change **Government** to **government**

    B. Change **selected** to **selected**

    C. Change **her** to **herself**

    D. Make no change

To do well on these tests, students are asked to draw upon exactly the skill they use when they ratiocinate. They look at the myriad possibilities and make the best choice based on meaning, based on context. In this sense their own writing becomes the mentor text for what they will find on a test. Those who have experienced ratiocination are not intimidated and go about answering such test items in a comfortable and authentic way. Ratiocination enables that.

Teaching Idea

We know ratiocination works. Take the idea from procedure and apply what students need. Think ZPD—Vygotsky's now famous Zone of Proximal Development—where are my students and where do I want them to be? Then design the codes, clues, and decodes accordingly. In the first edition of *Acts* we have ten codes ready for use, but there are as many possibilities as there are grammar concepts.

APPENDIX A

The 10 Basics of Diagramming

1. A horizontal line holds the subject, verb, predicate nominatives, predicate adjectives (subjective complements), appositives, direct objects, and objective complements. _____

2. A full vertical line separates the subject from the verb.

girl | plays

3. A half vertical line separates the verb from the direct object.

girl | plays | house

4. A slanted line separates the verb from predicate nominatives, and predicate adjectives.

Jim | is \ studious

5. An indirect object rests on a horizontal line attached by an empty diagonal line below the verb. Indirect objects have an indirect diagram.

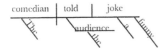

6. A backslash line separates the verb from objective complements.

They | called | her \ Midge

7. An appositive is placed in a parenthesis after the named subject.

Joe (the plumber) | died

8. All modifiers hang off the word they modify on a diagonal line.

9. Phrases hang off the word they modify on a diagonal line.

10. Compound elements get a fat arrow with the conjunction on a dotted line near the point.

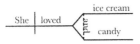

Other lines such as the upside down Y, zigzags, other angles, and dotted steps fit more complicated structures, but the 10 basics are a good starting place. For in-depth work on diagramming, try *Diagramming Step by Step: One Hundred and Fifty-five Steps to Diagramming Excellence* by Eugene R. Moutoux. For a delightful book about her experiences with diagramming peppered with history, try *Sister Bernadette's Barking Dog: A Quirky History and Lost Art of Diagramming Sentences* by Kitty Burns Florey.

REFERENCES

Belanoff, Pat, Betsy Rorschach, and Mia Oberlink. *The Right Hand-book.* Portsmouth, NH: Boynton/Cook, 1993.

Berlin, Irving. *Annie, Get Your Gun.* Broadway Musical, 1946.

Carroll, Joyce Armstrong. "Ratiocination and Revision, or Clues in the Written Draft." *English Journal* (November 1982): 90–92.

————. *Authentic Strategies for High-stakes Tests.* Spring, TX: Absey & Co., 2007.

————. *What Makes a Master Teacher.* Spring, TX: Absey & Co., 2008.

Carroll, Joyce Armstrong, and Edward E. Wilson. *Acts of Teaching.* Englewood, CO: Teacher Ideas Press, 1993.

————. *Acts of Teaching, How to Teach Writing.* 2nd ed. Westport, CT: Teacher Ideas Press, 2008.

Clark, Stephen. *A Practical Grammar.* 4th ed. Cincinnati, OH: H.W. Derby & Co., 1848.

Cutler, Charles. *The English Language: From Anglo-Saxon to American.* Middletown, CT: American Educational Publications, 1968.

Davis, Bette. *The Lonely Life: An Autobiography.* New York: G.P. Putnam's Sons, 1962.

Florey, Kitty Burns. *Sister Bernadette's Barking Dog: The Quirky History and Lost Art of Diagramming Sentences.* Hoboken, NJ: Melville House, 2006.

Goldstein, Alvin G., and June E. Chance. "Visual Recognition Memory for Complex Configurations," *Perception & Pyschophysics* 9-2B (1970): 237–241.

Grosholz, Emily R. "On Necklaces." In *The Best American Essays,* edited by Robert Atwan. New York: Houghton Mifflin, 2008.

Hart, John. *The Opening of the Unreasonable Writing of our Inglish Toung* [sic.], 1551.

Hartwell, Patrick. "Grammar, Grammars, and the Teaching of Grammar." *College English* (February 1985).

Johnston, Levi. "Me and Mrs. Palin." *Vanity Fair* (September 2, 2009).

Kaufman, George S. *Night at the Opera* (screenplay). New York: Viking, 1972.

Lamott, Anne. *Bird by Bird.* New York: Pantheon Books, 1994.

Leinstein, Madame. *The Good Child's Book of Stops: or, Punctuation in Verse.* London: Dean & Munday; A. K. Newman and Co., 1825.

Lincoln, Abraham. *The Words of Abraham Lincoln.* (Introduction by Larry Shapiro.) New York: Newmarket Press, 2009.

Livio, Mario. *The Golden Ratio.* New York: Broadway Books, 2002.

Lowth, Robert. *A Short Introduction to English Grammar.* London: Kessinger Publishing, 1762.

McGough, Roger. "Apostrophe." In *The Mersey Sound: Adrian Henri, Roger McGough and Brian Patten.* 3rd ed., A. Henri, R. McGough, and B. Patten. New York: Penguin Books, 1986.

Milne, A.A. *Winnie-the-Pooh.* New York: Dutton Children's Books, 2009.

Morris, Alana. *Vocabulary Unplugged.* Shoreham, VT: Discover Writing Press, 2005.

Moutoux, Eugene R. *A First Book of Sentence Diagramming.* Louisville, KY, 2004.

———. *A Second Book of Sentence Diagramming.* Louisville, KY, 2004.

———. *Diagramming Step by Step.* Louisville, KY, 2007.

Murray, Donald M. *A Writer Teaches Writing: A Practical Method of Teaching Composition.* New York: Houghton Mifflin, 1968.

Nims, John Frederick. *Western Wind.* New York: Random House, 1974.

Pulver, Robin. *Punctuation Takes a Vacation.* New York: Holiday House, 2003.

Reed, Alonzo, and Brainerd Kellogg. *Higher Lessons in English.* London: Kessinger Publishing, revised in 1887.

Rylant, Cynthia. *The Relatives Came.* New York: Bradbury Press, 1985.

Sandburg, Carl. *Chicago Poems.* Stilwell, KS: Digireads, 2008.

Swift, Jonathan. *Baucis and Philemon: A Poem. One the ever lamented Loss of the two Yew-Trees, In the Parish of Chilthorne, Near the County Town of Somerset. Together with Mrs. Harris's Earnest Petition.* London: H. Hills, in Black-fryars, near the Water-fide, 1709.

Wilde, Sandra. *You Kan Red This!* Portsmouth, NH: Heinemann, 1992.

Zimmer, Ben. "The Age of Undoing." *The New York Times Magazine* (September 20, 2009).

INDEX

Comma: adverb clause use, 109; complex sentence, 121; compound/complex sentences, 122; compound sentence, 120; conjunctive adverb, 86; coordinate adjective use, 155−56; cumulative adjective use, 156; function, 148; grammatical conventions, 6; interjection use, 88−89; nonrestrictive clause, 106; noun in direct address, 30; parenthesis use, 162; pedagogy, 146−47; quotation mark, 160; use, 152−55

Command sentence, 118

Comma splice, 155

Communication, 7, 139

Comparative degree, 46−47; adverb, 52; *little/littlest/least* problem, 49−50

Comparison: contrast in paragraphs, 139; *Gettysburg Address* analysis, 142−43; *then/than* problem, 85

Complement: adjective, 48; gerund phrase use, 97, 98; noun, 30

Complete sentence, 102

Complex sentence, 121−22

Composition: internal/external coherence of paragraphs, 137; paragraph punctuation, 135−36; paragraph unity, 137

Compound antecedent, 43

Compound noun, 24

Compound sentence, 120−21; complex sentence and, 121−22

Compound word, hyphen use, 160

Conclusion, writing of, 191

Conditionality: linking verb, 60; subjunctive mood, 73

Conjunction, 80−88; coordinating, 81−84, 105; correlative, 85−86; *like/as* problem, 87−88; subordinate clause, 108; subordinating, 84−85; *then/than* problem, 85

Conjunctive adverb, 86; semicolon use, 151−52

Connotation, 6, 13

Context: demonstrative pronoun use, 34−35; diagramming sentences, 127;

has/had/have in perfect tense, 68−69; knowledge test, 196−97; learning in, 4; *lie/lay* use, 65−66; meaning, 2; naming, 18; phrase/clause instruction, 113−14; phrase function, 97; predicate, 123; proofreading grammar knowledge, 195; relative clause, 110; sentence fragment, 126; sentence sense, 115; teaching grammar in, 3; verb tense time lines, 71; word meaning, 6, 16, 18, 20

Continuous action, 109

Contraction: apostrophe use, 156−57; it's/it problem, 43−44; *n't* with helping verb, 61

Contrary-to-fact conditional, 73

Conversational language, 81

Coordinate adjective, comma use, 155−56

Coordinating conjunction: comma use, 153; compound sentence, 120−21; *Gettysburg Address* analysis, 142−43; independent clause, 105; semicolon use, 151

Copula. *See* Linking verb

Copyrighted work capitalization, 171

Correctness: final prepositions, 81; literate acts, 4; *and* or *but* at start of sentence, 88

Couple (collective noun), 42−43

Courtesy rule for pronoun, 33−34

Cultural diversity, 6

Cumulative adjective, comma use, 156

Curly bracket. *See* Brace

Curriculum, 2, 175−76; eleventh grade writing, 188−94; fourth grade writing, 179−81; grammar-oriented writing, 194; parts of speech, 90; second grade writing, 177−78; seventh grade writing, 181−83; tenth grade writing, 184−86

Cutler, Charles, 6

D

Dangling modifier, 102−3

Dangling participle, 76

Dash: em, 161−62; en, 160−61; interjection use, 88

Dative case, 77

Davis, Bettie, 122, 123

Historical reference, capitalization, 170
Homograph, 14, 15
Homonym, 14–15
Homophone, 14
Hyphenated word capitalization, 169
Hyphen use, 160
Hypothetical conditional, 73

I
Idea, 24; paragraph planning, 136;
    paragraph unity and coherence, 137
Idiom, 16, 81
I/me use, 32–34
Imperative mood, 72–73
Imperative sentence, 9, 118
Incorrect grammar, 2; intensive pronoun, 40
Indefinite article, 55
Indefinite pronoun, 36
Indention: dialogue and quotation marks,
    160; *Gettysburg Address* analysis,
    143–44; paragraphs, 135, 136, 148;
    teaching exercise, 144–45
Independent clause, 104, 105; absolute,
    112; absolute phrase, 102; colon use,
    150–51; comma use, 153, 155; complex
    sentence, 121; compound/complex
    sentences, 121–22; compound sentence,
    120; coordinating conjunction, 81;
    prepositional object, 124; relative
    pronoun, 38; semicolon use, 151–52;
    simple sentence, 119–20
Indicative mood, 72–73
Indirect discourse punctuation, 149
Indirect object, 124
Inductive paragraphs, 138
Infinitive, 74–75; formation, 78; phrase,
    97; split, 5–6
Infix, 13
Inflected language, 6; preposition, 77
Insertion: bracket use, 163–64; quotation
    capitalization, 169–70
Intensifier: adjectival phrase, 100;
    exclamation point use, 150
Intension, 13

Intensive pronoun, 38–40
Interjection, 88–89; exclamatory sentence,
    118
Internalized pattern, 1; school grammar, 3
Internet, 19–21, 173
Interrogation mark. *See* Question mark
Interrogative pronoun, 36–37
Interrogative sentence, 117
Intransitive verb, 61–62; lie, 65
Introductory phrase, 181
Inverted comma. *See* Quotation mark
Irregular adjective, 47–48
Irregular plural noun, 27–28
Irregular verb: to be, 58; *lie/lay* problem,
    64–66
Is (linking verb), 59
Italic, 164–65, 165
It's/its problem, 43–44

J
Johnston, Levi, 34
Joiner, 120–21, 160
Joint, 150
Join word. *See* Conjunction

K
Kellogg, Brainerd, 127, 130

L
Label word. *See* Noun
Language: academic, 4; advertising, 138;
    awareness of grammar, 4; capitalization,
    171; capitalization of names of, 171;
    cognitive, 13; conversational, 81;
    curriculum and, 2; dynamic character
    and grammar, 6–7; effectiveness and
    power, 4; emotive, 13; English learners,
    63; formal, 2, 81; inflected, 6, 77;
    knowledge as power, 4; as living, 6–7;
    referential, 13; spoken and writing, 126;
    structural relationships, 3–4
"Languages" (Sandburg, Carl, poem), 7
Latin: *adiectivus,* 45; *antecedere,* 107;
    compositio, 135; *con-,* 80; *diathesis,* 71;

etymologia, 17; *imperare,* 118; irregular noun forms, 27; *italicus,* 164–65; *junct,* 80; *nomen,* 23; *paragraphus,* 136; *participialis,* 98; preposition, 77; *pro,* 31; *punctus,* 148; rhetorical voice, 71; *transitus,* 61

Lay use, 64–66

Learning grammar, 3–4; abstraction, 5; noun singular/plural forms, 28

Learning theory, 176

Leinstein, Madame, 146–47

Less/fewer problem, 48–49

Letters (correspondence), capitalization, 170

Lexeme, 12

Lie use, 64–66

Like/as problem, 87–88

Lincoln, Abraham, 140–44

Linguistics, 2; academic language, 4; grammar as meta-, 5

Linking verb, 59–61; *bad/badly* problem, 54; to be, 58; *good/well* problem, 54; predicates, 123

List punctuation: braces, 164; colon, 150–51; semicolon, 151

Literacy, 1, 4

Literary work punctuation, 165–66

Little/littlest/least problem, 49–50

Livio, Mario, 28

Loan word. *See* Borrowed word

Logic, 140, 145

Lowercase letters, 151, 157

Lowth, Robert, 81, 88

M

Magazine title punctuation, 165

Main clause, 104, 105; absolute phrase, 101–2; adverb clause punctuation, 109; fragment, 102; relative pronoun, 38

Masculine noun, 24

Master teacher, 5, 139–40

Mathieu, Joan, 33

May and *can,* 61

McGough, Roger, 157

Meaning: adjectival phrase, 100; borrowed words, 6; can/may, 61; communication of, 139; composition, 135; conjunction, 80; connotation/denotation, 13; context, 6, 16, 18, 20, 68–69; dynamic language, 6–7; grammar study and understanding, 7; grammatical function, 54; lay/lie, 65; lexeme, 12; *little* and adjective degree use, 49–50; morpheme, 12; paragraph, 135–36; preposition, 77; punctuation function, 148; relative clause context, 110; restrictive/nonrestrictive clause and sentence, 105–6; *sub-* as prefix, 84; *up,* 80; verb phrase, 99; verb voice, 71–72; word, 6, 12–13, 15–16, 18, 20

Memorization, 5, 48

Meta-language, 5

Metaphor: abstract thinking, 4–5; *as/like* problem, 88; diagramming sentences, 127; *like/as* problem, 88

Middle English, 5; *ethimologie,* 17; irregular noun forms, 27–28; *jonke,* 20; noun, 23; preposition, 77; pronoun gender, 32; *tens* in, 67

Miller, Dennis, 145

Milne, A. A., 149

Missing letter punctuation, 157

Mistake: colon insertion, 150–51; correction, 163–64; dangling modifier, 102–3; *it's/its,* 43; phrase fragment, 102, 110; verb/verbal confusion, 74

Mnemonic device: coordinating conjunction, 81; less/few problem, 48; subordinating conjunction, 84; tenth grade writing, 188

Mood of verb, 72–74

Morpheme, 12, 13

Morris, Alana, 14–15

Mr. Stops, 146, 147, 172–73

Murray, Donald, 135

Music name punctuation, 165

Myself use, 40

Myth of correctness, 81, 88

N

Naming word. *See* Noun

Narrative paragraph, 138

Necessary clause. *See* Restrictive clause

Neurological development, 5

Newspaper name punctuation, 166

Nominative absolute. *See* Absolute phrase

Nonrestrictive clause, 106; commas and, 155–56; relative, 107–8

Not, helping verb use, 60–61

Noun, 3; adjectival phrase, 100; adjective clause, 110; adjective function, 45; apposition, 29–30; articles with, 55; classes of, 23–25; complements, 30; direct address, 30–31; gerunds, 75; *good/well* problem, 54; infinitive phrase, 97; *like* usage, 87, 88; possessive, 29–30; preposition, 77, 78; prepositional phrase, 78, 101; preposition position, 78; singular/plural, 26–28; subjects of sentence, 122; subordinate clause function, 108; teaching strategy, 90; as verb, 8, 9

Noun clause, 110–12

Noun phrase, 95–96; adjectival phrase, 100; clause function, 110

Number: adjective, 45; agreement, 32, 39, 42; capitalization, 168; fewer, 48–49; hyphen use, 160; parenthesis use, 163

O

Object: agreement of pronoun, 32–34; gerund phrase use, 97, 98; infinitive phrase, 97; noun clause use, 111; phrasal preposition, 79; sentence structure, 123–24; six basic sentence, 124

Old English, 5; irregular nouns, 27–28; preposition, 77; pronoun gender, 32

Omission, 164

"On Big Happy" (comic strip), 28–29, 50, 51, 80, 118–19, 149–50

The Opening of the Unreasonable Writing of our Inglish Toung (Hart), 150

Opposition, 14

P

Paragraph: eleventh grade writing, 188; *Gettysburg Address* analysis, 140–44; grammar, 136–37; internal/external coherence, 137; placement, 139–40; planning and punctuation, 135–36; structural effectiveness, 138–39; teaching rhetoric of, 144–45; as thought chunk, 139; transition, 140; unity, 137; visual effectiveness, 138

Parallel constructions: correlative conjunctions, 85–86; eleventh grade writing, 189; paragraph transition, 140; punctuation function, 148; seventh grade writing, 183

Parenthesis: quotation marks, 159; use, 162–63

Participial phrase, 98–99; dangling, 76

Participle, 75–76; formation of, 98; perfect tense formation, 67; regular verb, 62; sentence completion, 102

Parts of speech, 8; clause, 108–12; phrase, 95–102; relationships and preposition, 77; teaching, 89–93; word classes, 18–19

Parts-to-whole paragraph, 138

Pascal, Blaise, 11

Passive voice, 71–72; *to be,* 58; *Gettysburg Address* analysis, 143

Past participle, 62–63; active/passive voice and, 72; formation, 75; participial phrases, 98

Past tense: because/since problem, 109–10; fourth grade writing, 180–81; irregular verb, 63–64; *lie/lay* problem, 65–66; perfect, 67–68; perfect progressive, 70; progressive, 69–70; regular verb, 62; second grade writing, 178

Pattern: formal language, 2; internalized, 1; noun singular/plural forms, 26–28

Pedagogy, 139; diagramming sentences, 127–29, 129–30; elementary level test, 195–96; fourth grade writing, 181;

reciprocal phrase, 40–41; reflexive, 38–40; relative, 37–38; teaching strategy, 93

Pronunciation: heteronyms, 15; indefinite articles and, 55

Proper noun, 24, 29; capitalization, 168, 170–71; comma use, 154; as verb, 8

Public speaking, 145

Pulver, Robin, 172

Punctuation, 104, 145–47; abbreviated names, 148; braces, 164; brackets, 163–64; comma, 6; commas and conjunctive adverb, 86; comma use, 30, 106, 109; ellipsis, 164; four functions, 147–48; interjection, 88–89; italics, 164–65; paragraphs as, 135–36; quotation mark use with, 159–60; semicolon use, 86; sentence definition, 116–17; sentence fragment, 125, 126; tenth grade writing, 186

Punctuation mark: four functions of, 148; period use, 148; proscriptive pedagogy, 146–47; quotation mark use, 148–49

Punctuation Takes a Vacation (Pluver), 172

Q

Quality, 24; conclusion in draft, 191–93; naming, 18; positive degree, 47

Question, 117; helping verb use, 61; interrogative and relative pronoun, 38; interrogative pronoun, 36–37

Question mark: interrogative sentence, 117; parenthesis, 163; pedagogy, 147

Quotation: capitalization, 168–69; colon use within, 151; ellipsis use, 164; insertion capitalization, 169–70

Quotation mark: function, 148; literary work name punctuation, 166; punctuation with, 159–60; use, 148–49, 157–58

R

Ratiocination, 176; eleventh grade writing, 191, 193–94; fourth grade writing, 179; grammar-oriented writing, 194–95;

second grade writing, 179; seventh grade writing, 181–82, 183; teaching idea, 197; tenth grade writing, 185, 188

"Ratiocination and Revision or Clues in the Written Draft" (Carroll), 176

Reader, 137, 143, 152

Reading, 47–48, 148, 167

Reciprocal pronoun, 40–41

Reed, Alonzo, 127, 130

References, 163

Referential language, 13

Reflexive pronoun, 38–40

Regular verb, 62–63

Relative clause, 107–8

Relative pronoun, 37–38; clause with, 110; noun clause, 110–11

Religious reference, 171

Renaming appositives, 29–30

Repetition, 137; paragraph transition, 140; passive voice, 143; persuasive we, 142

Restrictive clause, 105–6; adjective clause, 110; relative, 108

Rhetoric: Aristotelian, 4; *and* functions, 81–84; *Gettysburg Address* paragraph analysis, 140–44; paragraph elements, 136–40; paragraph planning, 135–36; parts of speech, 8; sentence definition, 117; sentence fragment, 125, 126; teaching, 144–45; thesis/antithesis construction, 194; visual and structural effectiveness, 137, 138–39; voice in, 71–72

Rhetorical device: allusion, 141–42, 145; comparison/contrast use, 142–43; cumulative adjective, 156; paragraph indention, 144; passive voice, 143; persuasive we, 142

Rodgers, Paul, 135, 145

Root words, 13

Rorschach, Betsy, 135

Rueter, Sara, 139–40

Rule: comma with adjective, 155–56; courtesy, 33–34; helping verb use with not, 60–61; *like/as* use, 87–88;

88; paragraph placement, 139–40; paragraph transition, 140; paragraph visual effective, 138; reciprocal pronoun phrase, 40–41; sentence ending with preposition, 81. *See also* Usage

Subject: absolute phrase, 101–2; active/passive voice and, 72; agreement of pronoun, 32–34; appositive phrase, 96; eleventh grade writing, 191–92; gerund phrase use, 97; imperative sentence, 118; interrogative pronoun, 37; linking verb and, 59; noun clause use, 111; relative pronoun, 38–39; sentence definition, 116; sentence structure, 122; six basic sentences, 124; *as* usage, 87, 88; verb agreement, 124–25

Subjective complements, 30

Subject/verb agreement, 124–25

Subjunctive mood, 72, 73–74

Subordinate clause, 108; complex sentence, 121; compound/complex sentences, 121–22; relative pronoun, 38; semicolon use, 152

Subordinate conjunction: clause, 108; complex sentence, 121; compound/complex sentences, 121–22

Suffix, 13; *-er* and *-est,* 52–53; *-d,* 62; *-ed,* 98; *-er,* 46, 47; *-est,* 47; *-ing,* 62, 97, 98; *-ly,* 51; participle formation, 75; plural, 26–28; regular verb formation, 62

Superlative degree, 47; adverb, 52; *little/littlest/least* problem, 50

Surname, comma use, 154–55

'S use, 157

Swift, Jonathan, 152–53

Synonym, 14

Syntax, 3; sentence definition, 116; six basic sentence, 124

T

Teacher, 123; Clark, Stephen, 127; diagramming sentences, 129; grammar teaching experience, 175–76; master, 5, 139–40

Teaching: ABC Book of Grammar project ideas, 9; action and existence verb ideas, 58–59; clauses, 112–14; diagramming sentences, 127; elementary level test, 195–96; grammar, 3; high school level test, 196–97; ideas, 3; Mr. Stops, 146, 147, 172–73; nouns and parts of speech, 89–93; paragraph grammar, 144–45; phrase, 112–14; punctuation, 146–47, 172–73; ratiocination, 197; sentence pop-up book idea, 130–33; strategy, 177; thought communication, 139; verb tenses, 70–71; words, 19–21; writing process and grammar, 175–76. *See also* Pedagogy

Tense, 67–71; fourth grade writing, 179–81; verb forms, 62

Tenth grade grammar-oriented writing, 184–86

Test: coding procedure, 176–77; elementary level, 195–96; high school level, 196–97; sentence length, 193; subject/verb agreement, 124–23; verb as linking or action, 54, 59–60

That use, 107–8

Thaves, Bob, 123

The (article), 55

Them-nyms, 14–15

Then/than problem, 85

Thesis/antithesis construction, eleventh grade writing, 194

Third person pronoun, 31–32

Thought, 139; em dash use, 161; grammar and abstract, 4–5; sentence, 115–17. *See also* Ratiocination

Time: *Gettysburg Address* analysis, 144; paragraph transition, 140; *then/than* problem, 85. *See also* Tense

Time line, 71

Title citation: capitalization, 168, 169; italics use, 165–66; quotation marks and, 158

To, infinitive/preposition formation, 75, 78, 97

W

Washington, Booker T., 6

Well/good problem, 54

Were (subjunctive), 73

Which, use, 108

While use, 108

White, E. B., 127

Whitehead, Alfred North, 176

Whole-to-parts paragraph, 138

Whom use, 124

Who use: adjective clause, 110; relative clause, 108

Who/whom use, 37, 74

Wilde, Sandra, 15

Williams, William Carolos, 36

Wilson, Edward E., 70

Wish statements, 73

Word, 11; coding systems, 18; division, 160–61; elemental units of, 12–13; etymology, 16–18; irregular noun forms, 27–28; meaning, 6, 15–16, 18, 20; order, 45–46. *See also* Prefix; Problem usage; Suffix

Word choice: adjectival phrase, 100; connotation/denotation, 13; eleventh grade writing, 188; *Gettysburg Address* analysis, 142–43; heteronyms, 15; paragraph unity, 137; second grade writing, 179. *See also* Usage

Word class. *See* Parts of speech

Writing, 3; diagramming sentences, 128; extraneous phrase, 103; grade-level grammar-oriented teaching, 177–94; grammatical conventions, 6; grapheme, 12; phrase/clause use instruction, 112–14; process of, 175–76; ratiocination as grammar-oriented, 194–95; spoken language and careless, 126; tightening wordy, 40–41, 72; verb voice, 72; wordy, 103, 106. *See also* Composition

Y

Y to *i,* add *es,* 26

Z

Zimmer, Ben, 8

About the Authors

JOYCE ARMSTRONG CARROLL (EdD, HLD) has taught most grade levels, was professor of English and Writing at McMurry University, and is co-director of Abydos Learning International, formerly the New Jersey Writing Project in Texas (NJWPT), with her husband Edward E. Wilson. Carroll has served as President of the Texas Council of Teachers of English Language Arts, served on the National Council of Teachers of English's Commission on Composition, and was Chair of NCTEs Standing Committee Against Censorship. She received an Honory Doctorate of Humane Letters from Georgian Court University and The Edmund J. Farrell Lifetime Achievement  Award in English/Lanaguage Arts from the Texas Council of Teachers of English/ Language Arts. Carroll has written numerous books for teachers such as *Dr. JAC's Guide to Writing with Depth, Authentic Strategies for High-stakes Tests, Phonics Friendly Books, Inspiring the Classics through Children's Literature, Math, Reading/Writing Connections* (forthcoming), plus hundreds of journal articles. Carroll co-authored with her husband Prentice Hall's *Writing and Grammar* series 6-12.

EDWARD E. WILSON is codirector of Abydos Learning International, formerly the New Jersey Writing Project in Texas (NJWPT), with his wife, Joyce Armstrong Carroll. Wilson has taught on the elementary, secondary, and junior college levels and is a member of NCTE, TCTELA, and ASCD. A poet, he co-edited *Poetry After Lunch* with Carroll and co-authored with her Prentice Hall's *Writing and Grammar* series 6-12. Wilson is also the owner of Absey & Co., and is a publisher committed to educational excellence and creative works of literary merit.

CPSIA information can be obtained
at www.ICGtesting.com
Printed in the USA
FSHW020255270521
81830FS